DANTE'S INFERNO

Dante's Inferno

TRANSLATIONS BY
TWENTY CONTEMPORARY POETS

Introduced by James Merrill
With an Afterword by Giuseppe Mazzotta
Edited by Daniel Halpern

THE ECCO PRESS

COPYRIGHT © 1993 BY THE ECCO PRESS
PREFACE COPYRIGHT © 1993 BY DANIEL HALPERN
INTRODUCTION COPYRIGHT © 1993 BY JAMES MERRILL
AFTERWORD COPYRIGHT © 1993 BY GIUSEPPE MAZZOTTA
ALL RIGHTS RESERVED

THE ECCO PRESS
100 WEST BROAD STREET
HOPEWELL, NJ 08525
PUBLISHED SIMULTANEOUSLY IN CANADA BY
PENGUIN BOOKS CANADA LTD., ONTARIO
PRINTED IN THE UNITED STATES OF AMERICA
DESIGNED BY PETER A. ANDERSEN
THE TEXT OF THIS BOOK IS SET IN MONOTYPE DANTE BY
MICHAEL AND WINIFRED BIXLER
FIRST EDITION

THIS BOOK HAS BEEN PUBLISHED IN A SIGNED LIMITED
EDITION BY ECCO EDITIONS.
VERSIONS OF SOME OF THESE CANTOS HAVE APPEARED IN
Antaeus, Bitter Harvest, AND *Ploughshares,*
WHOSE EDITORS ARE GRATEFULLY ACKNOWLEDGED.

LIBRARY OF CONGRESS
CATALOGING-IN-PUBLICATION DATA

DANTE ALIGHIERI, 1265–1321.
[INFERNO. ENGLISH]
VERSIONS OF DANTE'S INFERNO: TRANSLATIONS BY
20 CONTEMPORARY POETS / EDITED BY DANIEL HALPERN.
P. CM.
$24.95
I. HELL—POETRY. 2. DANTE ALIGHIERI, 1265–1321—
TRANSLATIONS INTO ENGLISH. I. HALPERN, DANIEL,
1945–   . II. TITLE.
PQ4315.2.H28   1993
851'.1—DC20   92-28061   CIP
ISBN 0-88001-291-9

CONTENTS

CONTENTS

PREFACE

THIS STORY BEGINS in Detroit. I no longer recall the restaurant, but I believe it was over a notable Sangiovese from Dante's Tuscany that the subject of the *Inferno* was raised. My dining companions that night were James Merrill and Peter Hooten. It was agreed, as I remember, that Ecco would publish a new version of Dante's *Inferno*, to be translated by a group of contemporary English-speaking poets.

A few months later I wrote to poets whose own poetry I respected and admired and whom I suspected had more than a passing interest in Dante. I asked if they would be willing to translate a part of the *Inferno*. Some of them were familiar with Italian; others were proven translators; but, finally, all were selected for the quality of their own poetry in English.

What started out as an enthusiastic and positive response turned into, for a majority of the translators, a sort of translation nightmare, paralleled only by that of Dante's travels through the underworld. Eventually all the poets arrived individually at a solution, a way of rendering their canto(s) into English—finding, as it were, their own Virgil for the work at hand—whether via terza rima, some echo of that prosodic sound, a modified rhyme scheme, blank verse, or free verse.

I don't believe there has ever been such a translation of Dante, employing so many poets to achieve the finished poem—twenty different poets working to give over Dante's narrative to the English reader. The *Inferno*, along with everything else it has represented for nearly seven hundred years, is one of Western literature's great adventure stories. At last, here at the end of the twentieth century, we have a translation that accentuates the excitement of Dante's travels in the netherworld: a narrative that remains always in the service of language, rendering the humor, hostility, and mood swings into a translation that, canto after canto, finds a novel poetic idiom through which Dante's dark itinerary flows and blossoms.

The idea behind this translation of the *Inferno* is to put one of our "sacred" texts back into the hands of the keepers of the language, the poets themselves. It is my hope that readers new to Dante will find a convincing and exciting tale of inner and outer exploration and, for the initiated, a Dante who speaks, in English, with a new lyrical power.

—Daniel Halpern

INTRODUCTION

OURS IS AN AGE of indefatigable (if not always great) translation. Poets far from fluent in Spanish or Persian are busily rendering Neruda and Rumi. No need to tempt fate: if foreign tongues fail us, we can get a workout on an English text. Harry Mathews once asked his workshop to translate a paragraph by Evelyn Waugh into American. A three-word sentence, "The evening passed," became, in one student's hands, "It got late." A winning solution, which bears out the lesson of centuries: masterpieces are timeless, but their translations date and thus need redoing. Therefore, despite the many fine versions of Dante in English—Longfellow and Binyon, Sinclair and Mandelbaum— we appear always to have room for one more. *One* more? Here in a single volume (as long as the reader is disposed to let the part stand for the whole) is the potential for *twenty* new translations of the Divine Comedy.

To most twentieth-century readers the *Inferno is* Dante. Ours is a culture where, in Auden's words, "the deadly sins / Can be bought in tins / With instructions on the label." Atonement and salvation can hardly compete with the vicarious complicity aroused by Francesca's narrative, or Ser Brunetto's, or Ulysses'. As we follow the pilgrim past a mysterious point he will not name (Satan's nonexistent genitalia?) upward into starlight, we leave behind much of that pity and terror awakened by the damned. Just as Donne is more popular in our classrooms than Herbert or Traherne, so "today's reader," perfectly at home in the hells of Lust and Anger and Greed, views as secondary worlds the purgatorial labor and the heavenly bliss that will reward it. Purgatory enough is here on the page, in the difficulty of getting at Dante's meaning, while the ravishments of his form, his images and wording, make for a Paradise we can ponder, like the sun reflected in a river, without going blind.

The *Inferno* is not only the most gripping, but, I suspect, the most contrived of the three Cantiche, if only for the great precedent that smooths its way: Virgil, that is, and through him Homer—an underworld of disaffected, prophesying, blood-lapping shades. In Dante's time personal testimony to the Almighty's wishes was an inspiring, if potentially dangerous, commonplace. St. Paul himself was "caught up into Paradise, and heard unspeakable words, which it is not lawful for a man to utter." (If only our TV evangelists agreed. . . .) A small, cynical voice in my ear wonders if St. Paul isn't making things easy for himself and proposes this more realistic interpretation of those last ten words: ". . . which only a poet greater than I could dream of giving utterance to." Paul, to be sure, knew languages but lacked—most visionaries do— Dante's poetic training, his mastery of secular forms, his fluency in the full range of possible diction. With an instrument in such splendid working order, Dante came as close as any poet ever has to God's word, that ineffable tongue beyond our own—unless we ourselves are its nouns and verbs—which continues on occasion to be the most expressive one yet invented by mankind.

Knowing his worth, Dante never postures, though here and there letting fly some proto-Baroque effect, like the double metamorphosis in Canto XXV. His earmarks are matter-of-factness and concision; he has, after all, so much to tell. He must use every means he can (zodiacal signposts, local or humble similes, glosses from philosophy and myth) to locate and focus his action as sharply as possible. Self-limited to these bare hundred cantos averaging a scant 140 lines apiece, he cannot afford to pad—he is likelier to break off, pleading no more room—let alone spell out connections for a torpid reader. Toward both these goals a verse form of his own invention serves him magnificently.

Asked for an example of terza rima, readers of English poetry will point first to Shelley's "Ode to the West Wind." Yet this beautiful plotless paean gives only the faintest notion of the form's energy and variety in the hands of its inventor. At the practical level it works as a No Trespassing sign, protecting the text. A copyist's pious interpolation or unthinking lapse would at once set off the alarm. At the level of pleasure no verse form *moves* so wonderfully. Each tercet's first and third line rhyme with the middle one of the preceding set and enclose the new rhyme-sound of the next, the way a scull outstrips the twin, already dissolving oar strokes that propel it. And at the level of meaning, just as rhymes interlock throughout a canto, so do incidents and images throughout the poem. For instance, the already mentioned black hole at the heart of Earth "rhymes" with the dazzling, atomic, all-engendering point far out in the Primum Mobile, round which the angelic orders revolve and upon which, says Beatrice, "the heavens and all nature are dependent." In microcosm, meanwhile, any given tercet dramatizes the triple structures explored by the whole, and the progress of the verse, which allows for closure only when (and because) a canto ends, becomes a version "without tears" of the pilgrim's own. Rendering here some lightning insight or action, there some laborious downward or upward clambering, the terza rima can as well sweeten the pill of dogmatic longueurs ("This keeps moving, it will therefore end") and frame with aching fleetness those glimpses of earth denied now to the damned and blest alike.

It is here, where form and temperament merge, that the translator's choice is crucial: how much to render of the original, how much to provide, from his own gifts, to make up for what is lost. In today's global village, a lot of poetry is written to *be* translated and its idiom at least partly determined by user-friendly versions, geared to "accessibility," from the great poets of cultures remote from the poet's own. Should stanzas and meters, and the strenuous syntax these make for, be swept aside in the process, no one seems much to mind. Yet with Dante, whose way with the line is as fanciful and patrician as Botticelli's, a reader may wonder if the challenge of composing fourteen thousand lines in an exacting form wasn't just as much the *Commedia's* raison d'être as the poet's need to depict his vision, and if a translator unwilling to meet this challenge on his own terms isn't wasting our time and his.

To labor the point a bit further, we all know the opening tercet of the *Commedia*:

> Midway life's journey I was made aware
> That I had strayed into a dark forest,
> And the right path appeared not anywhere.

This is Laurence Binyon, who is capable of far better things. The gratuitous "I was made aware" may be rationalized on the grounds that the

Commedia is a drama of consciousness, but the homophonic close of line three illustrates the steep cost of faithfulness to the original form. Here now is a recent version by Allen Mandelbaum:

> When I had journeyed half of our life's way,
> I found myself within a shadowed forest,
> for I had lost the path that does not stray.

Mandelbaum is not attempting terza rima throughout, merely making, at the poem's outset, a courteous gesture toward the form. But in so doing he comes up with a solution at once brilliant and probably unavailable without the pressure of a needed rhyme; his third line is, if not "better" than Dante's "*che la diretta via era smarrita*," more electric in its wording and the implications of its active verbs. Longfellow's version of this line—"For the straightforward pathway had been lost"—illustrates his great good sense in choosing unrhymed blank verse that allows him, throughout the poem, a priceless fidelity to Dante's word order and emphasis. His line, neither feebler nor flashier than the original, calls it uncannily to mind. The problem with most translators is their limited command of language—their own, I mean; they can always get help with the other. Hence the bright idea of asking some of our finest poets to weave this garland.

The value of the present volume is precisely the variety of solutions arrived at by these twenty voices. Some of them perform astonishing feats of traditional versification. Others forgo signaling the tercets in favor of stressing the unbroken narrative length; yet another cleverly reshapes each tercet's density into a lighter, beeswax hexagon. A prevailing impulse is to relax the strict metrical hold upon meaning, while preserving the *look* of the original. Some may please only portions of the crowd—solo barefoot impressions of an ensemble on point. But at best all are interesting, viable new species in the inexhaustible rain forest of *l'altissimo poeta*. Thanks to Dante's own variety of diction and to the rich layers of genre that make up the *Commedia* (Grandgent lists them as "the Encyclopedia, the Journey, the Vision, the Autobiography, the Praise of Woman, the Allegory"), this pluralistic approach seems natural enough. Dante's organizing presence, as interlocutor and witness, lends the urgency of identification throughout. (Is it absurd to detect his genes in such narrators of fantastic adventure as Arthur Gordon Pym and Ishmael?) Whatever Dante sees and hears he bears in mind, he takes to heart. Unlike any other epic poet I can think of, he has no hero to celebrate. It is his self-confessed frailty, his need for guidance, that draw us to him; and it is *this* translation, into the anonymous minds and hearts of each new generation of reader, to which these assembled by Daniel Halpern answer so eloquently. Many hands have made, in the present case, not light but lasting work.

—James Merrill

DANTE'S INFERNO

CANTO I / *Seamus Heaney*

In the middle of the journey of our life
   I found myself astray in a dark wood
   where the straight road had been lost sight of.
How hard it is to say what it was like
   in the thick of thickets, in a wood so dense and gnarled   5
   the very thought of it renews my panic.
It is bitter almost as death itself is bitter.
   But to rehearse the good it also brought me
   I will speak about the other things I saw there.
How I got into it I cannot clearly say   10
   for I was moving like a sleepwalker
   the moment I stepped out of the right way,
But when I came to the bottom of a hill
   standing off at the far end of that valley
   where a great terror had disheartened me   15
I looked up, and saw how its shoulders glowed
   already in the rays of the planet
   which leads and keeps men straight on every road.
Then I sensed a quiet influence settling
   into those depths in me that had been rocked   20
   and pitifully troubled all night long
And as a survivor gasping on the sand
   turns his head back to study in a daze
   the dangerous combers, so my mind
Turned back, although it was reeling forward,   25
   back to inspect a pass that had proved fatal
   heretofore to everyone who entered.
I rested a little then, for I was weary,
   then began to climb up the waste slopes once more
   with my firm foot always the lower one beneath me   30

When suddenly the spotted fluent shape
  of a leopard crossed my path
  not far up from the bottom of the slope,
Harrying me, confronting my advance,
  loping round me, leaping in my face   35
  so that I turned back downhill more than once.
The morning was beginning all above,
  the sun was rising up among the stars
  that rose with him when the Divine Love
First set those lovely things in motion,   40
  so I was encouraged to face with better hope
  the beast skipping in its merry skin
By the time of day, the sweetness of the season:
  but not enough not to be frightened by
  the sudden apparition of a lion   45
That came for me with his head in the air
  and so maddened by hunger that it seemed
  the air itself was bristling with fear.
And a she-wolf, so thin she looked as if
  all her appetites were gnawing at her.   50
  She had already brought many to grief
And I was so overcome at the sight of her
  my courage broke and I immediately lost heart
  in climbing the mountain any farther.
And as somebody who thinks he is going to win   55
  every time will be the most distressed one
  whenever his turn comes to be the loser—
I was like that as I retreated from
  the animal's turbulent head-on attack
  gradually, to where the sun is dumb.   60
While I was slipping back, about to sink
  back to the depths, I caught sight of one
  who seemed through a long silence indistinct.
When I saw him in that great waste land
  I cried out to him, "Pity me,   65
  whatever you are, shade or a living man."

He answered me, "No, not a living man
  though I was once alive, and had Lombards
  for parents, both of them Mantuan.
Although I was born *sub Julio*, my prime   70
  was spent in the heyday of the false gods
  when I lived in Rome, in good Augustus' time.
I was a poet, and I sang of that just son
  of Anchises who came out of Troy
  after the burning of proud Ilion.   75
But why do you face back into misery?
  Why do you not keep on up the sweet hill,
  the source and cause of all felicity?"
"Oh, are you then Virgil, are you the fountainhead
  of that wide river of speech constantly brimming?"   80
  I answered and for shame kept my head bowed.
"You are the light and glory of other poets.
  O let it avail me now, the long devotion
  that made me love your book and cleave to it.
You are my master, my authority.   85
  I learned from you and from you alone
  the illustrious style for which they honor me.
Look at the beast that has forced me to turn back.
  Help me, O famous sage, to confront her
  for she makes my veins race and my pulses shake."   90
"You will have to go another way around,"
  he answered, when he saw me weeping,
  "to escape the toils and thickets of this ground;
Because this animal you are troubled by
  lets no man pass but harasses him   95
  until she kills him by her savagery,
And she is so consumed by viciousness
  that nothing fills her, and so insatiable
  that feeding only makes her ravenous.
There are many animals she couples with   100
  and there will be more of them, until the Hound
  shall come and grind her in the jaws of death.

He will not glut himself on ground or riches,
    but wisdom, love, and virtue will sustain him
    and the two Feltros will vie to be his birthplace. 105
To humble Italy, for which the virgin
    Camilla died bleeding, and Turnus died, and Nisus
    and Euryalus, he will bring salvation.
He will pursue the wolf through every town
    until he has hunted and hounded her to hell 110
    where envy unleashed her first and set her on.
Therefore, for your own good, I think the best course
    is to follow me and I will be your guide
    and lead you from here through an eternal place
Where you will hear desperate screaming and will see 115
    those long-lost spirits in torment suffering
    the second death in perpetuity.
And then you will see those who are not distressed
    in the fire because they hope to come,
    whenever their time comes, among the blessed. 120
If you want to ascend among these, then you
    will be guided by a soul worthier than I
    and I will leave you with her when I go;
For that Emperor above does not allow
    me or my like to come into His city 125
    because I was a rebel to His law.
His empire is everywhere but His high seat
    and city are there, in His proper kingdom.
    O happy is the man He calls to it."
And I said to him, "I ask you, poet, 130
    in the name of that God you were ignorant of
    and to help me to escape my own worst fate,
Lead me to that place described by you
    so that I may see St. Peter's Gate
    and those other ones you spoke of in their sorrow." 135
Then he set off and I began to follow.

CANTO II / *Seamus Heaney*

Daylight was going and the umber air
   soothing every creature on the earth,
   freeing them from their labors everywhere:
I alone was girding myself to face
   the ordeal of the journey and my duty   5
   which literal memory will now retrace.
Now, O muses, and now, high genius, help me.
   And memory, that recorded what I saw,
   be manifest in me, sheer faculty.
"Poet," I began, "who are my guide,   10
   consider what my strength is able for
   before you set me on the arduous road.
You tell how the father of Silvius
   went into eternity and was there
   in the living flesh, with all his bodily senses,   15
And yet the thoughtful man will understand
   why the Adversary of all things evil,
   considering the greatness he would found
And who and what spring from him, showed him favor—
   for he was chosen in the empyrean   20
   to father glorious Rome and her empire
And we cannot speak of Rome or of the empire
   truly, except as the holy seat
   founded to keep great Peter's successor.
On that journey, celebrated by your skill,   25
   he was enlightened and set upon the way
   toward victory and the papal mantle.
Then the Chosen Vessel went there and returned
   with confirmation of that faith which is
   the beginning of the way into salvation.   30

But I, why should I go? Who grants me passage?
  I am not Aeneas and I am not Paul.
  My unworthiness is plain for all to judge.
Therefore, were I to undertake this journey
  I fear it would be madness. But you are wise.   35
  What I can hardly grasp, you know completely."
And like a man reneging his decision,
  having second thoughts and shifting ground,
  withdrawing from the course he has embarked on,
On that dark hillside there and then I weakened   40
  for once I admitted doubts about a purpose
  so hastily conceived, the purpose went.
"If I have understood you rightly in this,"
  the shade of that magnanimous soul replied,
  "your spirit is being plagued by cowardice   45
Which often weighs on a man, makes him distrust
  an honorable course and turns him from it
  as seeing wrong will turn a shying beast.
So to rid you of this fear, I will tell you
  why I have come and everything I've heard   50
  from the moment I began to care for you.
I was among those who are in suspense
  when a lady called me, so blessed and beautiful
  I pleaded with her to let me do her service.
Her eyes were shining brighter than the stars   55
  and she began to speak with an angel's voice
  in that gentle and quiet speech of hers:
'O courteous spirit of Mantua, whose fame
  is lasting in the world, and for as long
  as the world endures will always last the same,   60
My friend—no friend of fortune's—on his trek
  up the desolate slope is so overcome
  and panic-stricken that he has turned back
And from the news I heard of him in heaven
  he may already be so far astray   65
  that I have roused myself too late to help him.

Hurry to him, speak in your eloquent way
   and do whatever else is necessary
   to help him through, and that will comfort me.
I am Beatrice who am sending you.   70
   I come from the place I am yearning to return to.
   It was love that moved me and love makes me speak.
When I am in the presence of my Lord
   I will talk about you often and every word
   will praise you.' She was silent then and I began,   75
'O lady of virtue, through you and you alone
   mankind surpasses all that is contained
   within the close sphere of the circling moon.
To do your bidding gratifies me so
   that were it done already, it would be late.   80
   Your will is my will, you need only say.
Yet tell me also why it holds no terror
   for you to descend here into this deep center
   out of that spacious zone you are homesick for.'
'Since you are so penetrating and eager   85
   for knowledge,' she answered, 'I will tell you briefly
   why I am not afraid to enter here.
Only things with the power to do harm
   deserve our fear, and those things alone—
   nothing else, for nothing else is fearsome.   90
I am not subject to your misery
   because God, by His grace, made me immune
   and none of the flames burning here afflicts me.
In heaven above there is a gentle lady
   so concerned for the vexed soul I commit to you   95
   that the stern judgment has been eased on high.
And this lady was moved to intercede
   with Lucy, saying, "I commend your faithful one
   to you, who is sorely beset now and in need."
And Lucy, who abhors all cruelty,   100
   arose and made her way to where I was
   seated in ancient Rachel's company.

"You, Beatrice," she said, "true praise of God,
   why won't you help the man who loved you so
   that for your sake he broke from the common crowd?   105
Do you not hear the sorrow in his cry?
   Do you not see the death assailing him
   on that water which outsways the very sea?"
Nobody with more alacrity
   ever sought the advantage or fled harm's way   110
   than I, when I had heard these speeches uttered,
Sought to come down here from my heavenly seat
   and put my whole trust in your noble language
   which honors you and everyone who hears it.'
When she had finished persuading me   115
   she turned her eyes away, shining with tears,
   so I yearned the more to come, and accordingly
Did come to you because of her reasons
   and took you out of the path of that wild beast
   which barred the short way to the lovely mountain.   120
What is it, then? Why are you hesitating?
   Why do you let cowardice skulk inside your heart?
   Why are you not daring and liberated
When three such blessed ladies have sued
   on your behalf in the court of heaven   125
   and my own words to you promise so much good?"
As little flowers, which were all bowed and shut
   by the night chills, rise on their stems and open
   as soon as they have felt a touch of sunlight,
So I revived in my own wilting powers   130
   and my heart was flushed up with such bravery
   that I began like somebody set free:
"Oh, what compassion she had who relieved me!
   And what courtesy you have who obeyed
   all her true intercession so quickly.   135
What you have said has turned my heart around
   so much that I am as ready to come now
   as I was before I started losing ground.

Go on, then, for one will informs us both.
   You are my guide, my master and my teacher."   140
   This is what I said, and when he moved
I entered on the deep and savage path.

CANTO III / *Seamus Heaney*

THROUGH ME IT LEADS TO THE CITY SORROWFUL.
  THROUGH ME IT LEADS TO THE ETERNAL PAIN.
  THROUGH ME IT LEADS AMONG THE LOST PEOPLE.
JUSTICE INSPIRED MY MAKER ABOVE.
  IT WAS DIVINE POWER THAT FORMED ME,   5
  SUPREME WISDOM AND ORIGINAL LOVE.
BEFORE ME NO THING WAS CREATED EXCEPT THINGS
  EVERLASTING. AND I AM EVERLASTING.
  LEAVE EVERY HOPE BEHIND YOU, YOU WHO ENTER.
I saw these words inscribed above a gate   10
  in obscure characters; and so I said,
  "Master, I find their sense hard to interpret."
And he said to me like one experienced,
  "All your distrust must be abandoned here,
  here and now all cowardice must be ended.   15
We have come to the place I told you to expect,
  where you would see that people in their sorrow
  who have forfeited the good of intellect."
And he put his hand on my hand then
  with a glad look on his face which soothed me   20
  as he led me in to the realm of things hidden.
Here sighing and laments and wailing cries
  went harrowing the air where no stars shone
  so that at first the tears came to my eyes.
A garble of languages, high baying sounds,   25
  beseeching cadences, surges of rage,
  screeches and moans and the plash of beating hands
Made pandemonium which does not relent
  but keeps that darkened and timeless element
  in turbulence, like sand in a whirlwind.   30

Horror reeled round my head and ringed me in
  so that I said, "Master, what am I hearing?
  Who are these people who seem so lost to pain?"
And he said to me, "Such are the sorrows
  undergone by the stricken souls of those   35
  whose lives were lived without disgrace or praise.
They belong here with that choir of angels,
  the cowardly ones, self-seekers, self-preservers,
  who did not stand with God yet were not rebels.
Heaven banished them, to keep its beauty pristine,   40
  and deep hell does not admit them, in case the wicked
  might show the fairer by comparison."
And I asked him, "Master, what kind of affliction
  do they suffer, they lament so bitterly?"
  And he, "I will explain it to you briefly.   45
These ones do not have any hope of death,
  and their life is so blind and abased that they envy
  every other fate that souls can meet with.
The world lets no report of them survive.
  Both Mercy and Justice hold them in disdain.   50
  Let us not talk of them. Move on. Observe."
And as I looked again I saw a banner
  swirling and swept about at such great speed
  it seemed compelled to shift like that forever,
And behind it such a long procession   55
  of people, I should never have believed
  death had brought so many to their ruin.
Among them there were ones I could recognize
  and when I saw and knew the shade of him
  who made the great refusal through cowardice   60
Immediately there and then it came to me
  that this was the useless crew who are repugnant
  not just to God, but to God's enemies even.
These unfortunates, whose lives were without life,
  went naked and were stung unmercifully   65
  by hornets and wasps that the place was swarming with;

Their faces bled; the blood ran down in streams
   that mixed with tears and fell about their feet
   where it was ingested by repulsive worms.
Then, when I looked a bit ahead, I saw   70
   people on the shore of a great river
   and so I said to him, "Now, Master, will you
Instruct me about them and what it is dictates
   their readiness to cross over, or what seems
   like readiness to me in this dim light?"   75
"To you, these things are going to be plain,"
   he answered, "the moment you set foot
   on the sad riverbank of Acheron."
Then, because I feared my words displeased him,
   I walked on with a downcast, shamefaced look   80
   and until we reached the river I did not speak.
And there in a boat that came heading toward us
   was an old man, his hair snow-white with age,
   bawling out, "Woe to you, wicked spirits!
Never hope to see the heavenly skies.   85
   I come to bring you to the other shore,
   to eternal darkness, to the fire and ice.
And you there, you, the living soul, separate
   yourself from these others who are dead."
   But when he saw that I did not stand aside   90
He said, "By another way, by other harbors
   you shall reach a different shore and pass over.
   A lighter boat must be your carrier."
And my guide said, "Quiet your anger, Charon.
   There where all can be done that has been willed   95
   this has been willed; and there can be no question."
Then straightaway he shut his grizzled jaws,
   the ferryman of that livid marsh,
   who had wheels of fire flaming round his eyes.
But as soon as they had heard the cruel words,   100
   those lost souls, all naked and exhausted,
   changed their color and their teeth chattered;

They blasphemed God and their parents on the earth,
   the human race, the place and date and seedbed
   of their own begetting and of their birth,   105
Then all together, bitterly weeping, made
   their way toward the accursed shore that waits
   for every man who does not fear his God.
The demon Charon's eyes are like hot coals fanned.
   He beckons them and herds all of them in   110
   and beats with his oar whoever drops behind.
As one by one the leaves fall off in autumn
   until at length the branch is bared and sees
   all that was looted from it on the ground,
So the bad seed of Adam, at a signal   115
   pitch themselves from that shore one by one,
   each like a falcon answering its call.
They go away like this over the brown waters
   and before they have landed on the other side
   upon this side once more a new crowd gathers.   120
"My son," the courteous master said to me,
   "all those who die under the wrath of God
   come together here from every country
And they are eager to go across the river
   because Divine Justice goads them with its spur   125
   so that their fear is turned into desire.
No good spirits ever pass this way
   and therefore, if Charon objects to you,
   understand well what his words imply."
When he had ended, such a violent tremor   130
   shook the dark plain I still run with sweat
   at the very memory of my terror.
The tear-soaked ground blew up a wind
   that went foundering and flaring and flashed crimson
   so that all my faculties were stunned   135
And I fell like a man whom sleep has overcome.

CANTO IV / *Mark Strand*

A heavy crack of thunder broke
   upon the deepest currents of my sleep,
   so that suddenly I woke
As if by force, and with a drowsy gaze
   looked about, then stood   5
   to get a better sense of where I was,
And found myself at the edge of a steep rise
   that dropped into an abyss of pain,
   a vale of endless cries,
So clogged with murky air,   10
   so dark, that though I strained to see
   into its depths, I saw nothing there.
"Let's descend to that blind world below,"
   began the poet, his face like ash,
   "I'll go first, and you can follow."   15
But when I saw how scared, how pale
   he was, I said, "How can I count on you
   to help me if I should fail?"
And he to me, "It's the people here,
   their misery that paints my face   20
   with the pity you mistake for fear.
Come, a long way lies ahead of us."
   He entered, and had me enter too
   the first circle surrounding the abyss.
There was no howling that I could hear,   25
   nothing but sighs that rose
   to shake the everlasting air,
Sighs of painless woe
   from milling crowds of men and women
   and children who would never know   30

Relief. Then the good master said, "Don't you care
  whose souls these are you see?
  Before we travel anywhere,
Know they have not sinned, that all their good
  was not enough. Baptism alone   35
  is the gate to the faith you hold,
And if they lived before the days
  of Christianity, they did not
  truly worship God: I am one of these.
For this fault only, and no other crime,   40
  we are lost, and our punishment is to live
  without hope until the end of time
Yet with desire." On hearing this a sadness filled
  my heart for all the noble souls
  who now in limbo dwelled.   45
"Tell me, Master, tell me," I began,
  wanting to be sure of the faith
  that overcomes all wrongs, "Has anyone
Ever left this place
  on his own merits, or on another's, who later on   50
  was blessed?" And he, able to guess
My meaning, answered, "I was new here
  when I saw a mighty lord appear,
  wearing a crown of victory.
And he led away our first father's shade,   55
  and his son Abel's, and Noah's,
  and that of trusting Moses who made
The laws; and patriarchal Abraham,
  and David the king, and Israel with his father
  and children, and Rachel, who resisted him,   60
And many others, and he blessed them all.
  And you should know that before these
  not a human soul had yet been saved."
We did not stop, but walked with ease
  the while he spoke, passing through woods,   65
  woods, that is, of souls that stood like trees;

We still had not gone far from where I woke
   when I saw a fire in front of us,
   a glowing hemisphere that lit the dark.
We were still a short ways off   7
   but close enough to tell
   that worthy people gathered there.
"O you who honor science and art,
   who are these whose virtue is so great
   that from others they are kept apart?"   7
And he to me, "Each holds a place
   of honor in your world, which favors
   them down here, by Heaven's grace."
And while he spoke, another voice broke in,
   "Hail the greatest of poets, his shade   8
   that left is back with us again."
And when the voice was still,
   I saw four mighty shades come toward us,
   looking neither sad nor joyful.
"The one with sword in hand,"   8
   my master started to explain, "the one
   leading the other three and in command
Is Homer, the undisputed king
   of poets, and next is Horace the satirist,
   Ovid is third, with Lucan following.   9
Since they share with me a calling,
   the one just uttered by that voice,
   they do me honor, and honor what we do."
So before me stood that brilliant school
   led by the maker of the greatest poem,   9
   who soars above the others like an eagle.
After they talked among themselves awhile,
   they turned and welcomed me.
   At this, I saw my master smile.
They showed me even greater honor when   10
   they welcomed me as one of them,
   making me sixth among the wise.

And so we went together toward the light,
   talking of things best not spoken of again,
   as speaking of them once was right.   105
Then we arrived at the foot
   of a noble castle circled seven times
   by lofty walls, and guarded by a lovely moat,
Which we crossed as if on solid ground,
   then went through seven gates   110
   into a fresh meadow where we found
People with grave, slow-moving eyes,
   who bore the look of great authority,
   who seldom spoke and did not let their voices rise.
Then we moved to one side of a wide lawn,   115
   high and light-filled, from which
   those gathered there could be gazed upon.
There, before me, on that shining green,
   the great spirits were pointed out,
   and in my heart I felt the glory of the scene.   120
I saw Electra standing with a group
   among whom I saw Hector and Aeneas,
   and hawk-eyed Caesar, dressed for war.
I saw Camilla and Penthesilea,
   and seated across the lawn I saw   125
   King Latinus with Lavinia his daughter.
I saw Brutus, who drove away the Tarquin;
   Lucretia, Julia, Marcia, and Cornelia;
   and standing by himself, saw Saladin.
When I raised my eyes a little higher,   130
   I saw the master of those who know,
   sitting with his philosophic family
Who look his way and pay him honor.
   There, nearest him, and before the rest,
   I saw Socrates and Plato;   135
And Democritus, who says we're ruled by randomness,
   Diogenes, Anaxagoras, and Thales,
   Empedocles, Zeno, and Heraclitus;

I saw Dioscorides, the good taxonomist
   of plants, and I saw Orpheus,   140
   Tully and Linus, and Seneca the moralist;
Euclid the geometer, and Ptolemy,
   Hippocrates, Galen, Avicenna,
   and Averroës who made the Commentary.
I cannot stop to describe them all in full,   145
   for I am driven forward by my theme,
   and there is always more to say than I can tell.
The company of six shrinks to only two:
   my knowing guide leads me away,
   out of the quiet, into the trembling air.   150
And I come to a place where nothing shines.

CANTO V / *Daniel Halpern*

Then I went down through the first circle
   into the second, which encircles less space
   but a suffering so great it raises a chorus of weeping.
And that's where Minos stands, smiling grotesquely
   at the entrance where he looks over the souls,   5
   judges and sends them on, coiling his tail.
I mean to say, when the unfortunate soul
   appears before him, it confesses everything,
   and he, a connoisseur of mortal sins,
Knows exactly where each soul belongs in Hell.   10
   He coils himself with his tail, once for each
   of the levels down which that soul must descend.
There's always a crowd of them before him,
   and each, when its time comes, receives judgment.
   They speak, hear their fate, and are cast below.   15
"You who arrive in this house of pain,"
   cried Minos when his eyes discovered me,
   interrupting the work of his important office,
"Be cautious as you enter and whom you trust.
   Don't be fooled by the gate's easy entrance!"   20
   And my guide replied, "Must you too call out?
Don't get in the way of what's destined here,
   a journey willed from above by the One
   whose desires aren't questioned. Ask no more."
And now I begin to hear   25
   notes of misery. I find myself
   where a surfeit of weeping beats on me.
I came to a place of muted light,
   a place roaring like the sea pitched in a storm,
   torn apart by clashing winds.   30

The nightmarish, never-ending hurricane
    drives the spirits before it with a vengeance:
    whirling and punishing, tormenting them.
When they confront the storm-ripped landscape
    there are cries, weeping and lamentations,   35
    and it's there they curse God himself.
I learned this was the cruel punishment
    of the carnal sinners, those
    who abandon reason for desire.
And as starlings carry through winter air   40
    on wings in flocks crowded and wide,
    that wind bears the wicked spirits:
Here, there, up and down, driving them everywhere.
    There's no hope, nothing to console them,
    no chance of rest, much less of easing their pain.   45
And just as cranes fly, chanting their cries
    from extended formations of themselves,
    so the shades approached, wailing, keening,
Carried on that chaos of battling winds.
    I asked, "Master, who are these souls   50
    punished in the lash of this black air?"
"The first one whose story you wish to know,"
    he said, hearing my question, "was an empress
    who ruled a population of different tongues.
Such was her taste for promiscuity   55
    she passed laws condoning lust
    to justify her own scandal.
She is Semiramis, who, as we've read,
    was the wife of Ninus and succeeded him,
    and so ruled the land the Sultan now rules.   60
The spirit who came next killed herself for love
    and betrayed the ashes of Sichaeus.
    Next comes Cleopatra, driven by lust.
And Helen, responsible for years
    of savage war. And there's Achilles himself,   65
    who in his final battle lost to love.

See Paris, and Tristan!" He pointed out
   more than a thousand shades, naming each
   who for love alone was taken from the living.
As soon as I heard my teacher name   70
   the ladies and knights of another era,
   pity gripped me and set my mind adrift.
"Poet," I said to him, "I'd be happy
   to talk with those two who approach together,
   carried almost weightless on the wind."   75
And he said to me, "You'll see when they get
   closer to us. Then you can appeal to them
   by the love that bears them on, and they'll come to you."
At that moment the wind swept them near us
   and I called out, "Weary souls, come talk with us   80
   unless there's someone who forbids it!"
Just as doves, called down by desire,
   return with their wings poised and balanced
   through the air, willed back to their sweet nests,
Those two abandoned Dido's group,   85
   moving toward us through the malignant air—
   so convincing was my tender call to them.
"O living creature, gracious and kind,
   you have traveled here through this murky air
   to visit us who stained the world with blood.   90
If He who rules the universe were a friend
   we'd beg Him to grant you peace
   because you've pitied our depraved state.
Whatever you wish to hear we'll tell you,
   if you want to talk, we'll listen,   95
   for as long as it's windless here.
I was born in a town set on the shores
   where the Po and its tributaries
   converge, where their waters finally rest.
Love, which quickly ignites the tender heart,   100
   seized his heart with the beauty of my body,
   a beauty torn from me in an act that torments me still.

Love, which pardons no one who's loved from loving,
    took hold of me with a passion so strong
    it hasn't faded, as you can see for yourself.   105
Love guided us to a single death,
    but Caina awaits the one who took our lives."
    This was the speech they delivered to us.
What I heard from these wounded souls
    bent down my head, and I kept it lowered   110
    until the poet asked, "What are you thinking?"
I answered him by saying, "Alas,
    How many sweet thoughts, what great longing
    carried them to such a pathetic end!"
Then I again turned back to the lovers   115
    and said, "Francesca, everything you've suffered
    torments me with grief and pity.
But tell me, during those days of sweet sighs
    how did love make it possible for you
    to sense your sleeping passion?"   120
And she said to me, "There's no greater pain
    than remembering joy in a time
    of sorrow, as your teacher well knows.
However, if you really want to hear
    the story of how our love took hold,   125
    I'll tell you, weeping as I talk.
One day with nothing better to do we read
    of Lancelot, how he fell prey to love.
    We were alone, but suspected nothing.
As we read it happened our eyes would meet,   130
    draining the warm color from our faces.
    But it was a single passage that released us.
When we read how the long-pursued smile
    was kissed by so accomplished a lover,
    this man, who will be with me forever,   135
Kissed my mouth, his body trembling in the kiss—
    both the book and author our Gallehault.
    And so our reading ended for that day."

As she shared her story with me
   the other spirit wept. Pity struck me   140
   and I fainted, as if departing this life,
And down I went, as a dead body falls.

CANTO VI / *Galway Kinnell*

When I regain my senses that left me
　　at the piteous sight of those two relatives
　　which stunned me with sadness
I see new torments and tormented ones
　　all around me whichever way　　　　　　　　　　5
　　I move or turn or look.
I am in the third circle, place of eternal
　　accursed, cold and thudding rain
　　which in density and force is never new.
Large hailstones, dirty rainwater, and snow　　　10
　　course down through the murky air,
　　the ground that receives them stinks.
That cruel and strange creature Cerberus
　　who has three throats barks like a dog
　　over the people who wallow here.　　　　　　　15
Its eyes are red, its beard greasy and black,
　　its belly thick, its hands clawed,
　　it rips the spirits, skins and dismembers them.
The rain makes them howl like dogs,
　　with one side they make a screen for the other,　20
　　they turn over often, these profane sufferers.
When the great dragon Cerberus noticed us
　　it opened its mouths and showed its fangs,
　　it did not have a limb that it held still.
My guide spread his hands open wide　　　　　　25
　　and took up some earth and with full fists
　　threw it into those eager holes.
Just as a dog which yelps when it craves
　　becomes quiet when snapping up its food,
　　straining and battling to devour it,　　　　　　30

So became the soiled faces
 of the demon Cerberus that dins
 the spirits so they wish they were deaf.
We passed over the shades which the hard rain
 beats down, stepping upon   35
 their emptiness as if on bodies.
They were all lying on the ground
 except for one which sat up the moment
 it saw us passing in front of it.
"O you who are led through this inferno,"   40
 it said to me, "recognize me if you can,
 you were made before I was unmade."
And I said to him, "The anguish you are in
 perhaps removes you from my memory
 so that it does not seem I have ever seen you, 45
But tell me who you are, set down
 in this sorry place under such a penalty
 that if any is greater none is as repulsive."
He said to me, "Your city so filled
 with envy that its sack of it spills over   50
 held me within it in the cloudless life.
Your citizens called me Pigface
 for the damning fault of gluttony,
 as you see I lie battered under the rain.
And I, sad soul, am not alone   55
 for all these others are under the same penalty
 for the same offense." And he stopped.
I answered, "Ciacco, your anguish
 lies so heavily on me I could weep
 but if you know tell me what will happen 60
To the citizens of the divided city
 and if anyone in it is just and why
 it has been beset by so much discord."
And he said to me, "After long contending
 there will be bloodshed and the rustic party 65
 will drive out the other with much brutality.

Within three years this party in turn
    will fall and the other prevail
    through the force of one who now plays both sides.
That party will hold its head high a long time   70
    keeping its rival under heavy burdens
    however much it weeps and feels its shame.
Two are just and they are ignored,
    pride, envy, and avarice
    are the three sparks that inflame all hearts."   75
Here he put an end to his grievous report
    and I said to him, "I wish you would teach me more
    and make me the gift of further speech.
Farinata and Tegghiaiao who were so upright,
    Jacopo Rusticucci, Arrigo and Mosca   80
    and the others who set their minds to do good,
Tell me where they are, let me know of them
    for a strong desire seizes me to learn
    if heaven sweetens or hell embitters them."
And he said, "They are among the foulest souls,   85
    different sins weigh them toward the bottom,
    if you go down that far you may see them,
But when you are again in the sweet world
    I pray you to restore me to people's memory,
    more I will not say nor will I answer you."   90
At this he twisted his gaze askance,
    peered at me a moment then dropped his head
    and fell with it back among the other blind.
And my guide said to me, "He will not wake
    until the sounding of the angel's trumpet   95
    when the adverse power shall come
And the dead shall revisit their sad graves
    and resume their flesh and form
    and hear what resounds through eternity."
So we made our way across the dirty sludge   100
    of shades and rain with slow steps
    touching a little on the future life,

Of which I said, "Master, will these torments
   increase after the great sentencing
   or be less or be just as bitter?"   105
And he said, "Go back to your philosophy
   which tells that the more complete a thing is
   the more it feels its pleasure but also its pain.
Although these accursed people certainly
   will never come to true completion   110
   probably they will be closer to it then than now."
We wound along the turnings in the road
   saying much more than I tell here
   and came to the point where it slopes down.
Here we found Plutus, the great enemy.   115

CANTO VII / *Cynthia Macdonald*

"Pape Satan, pape Satan, aleppe!,"
　　said Plutus, babbling in a voice so coarse
　　it frightened me. Of course, my gentle guide
Knew how to reassure me: "Do not allow
　　your fear to gnaw at you; he cannot force　　　　5
　　us off the path we follow down this rock."
Then he turned back to Plutus' puffy face
　　and said, "Stop there, demonic wolf, consume
　　your skin and bones, ingest your fleshy rage.
Heaven has sent us to these somber realms　　　　10
　　to follow in the footsteps of the doomed,
　　those angels Michael vanquished and cast down."
As sails belled out by wind collapse and fall
　　into a heap of cloth when the mainmast breaks
　　so that satanic beast fell at our feet.　　　　15
We left, descending down the fourth incline
　　and saw ahead a barren, salty lake
　　where all the evils of the spheres are banked.
Justice of God! Who crammed into one sack
　　those dreadful penalties I saw? Who gave　　　　20
　　us spoils of guilt, then stuffed them down our throats?
As in Charybdis whirlpool's sucking mouth
　　each wave explodes against another wave,
　　so spirits danced, recoiled, and counterdanced.
On every side were even greater crowds　　　　25
　　than I had seen before. All howled and strained
　　their chests to muscle weights ahead.
They crashed and crashed again into each other,
　　screaming as they wheeled back to clash again:
　　"Why did you hoard it?" "Why did you throw it away?"　　30

They versed and reversed around that misery
   hurrying left or right for the riposte:
   to hurl their shameful questions back and forth;
No shift, no strategy, no changed direction
   deterred their circling back for the next jousts.   35
   My heart seemed punctured by each fresh assault.
I said, "Good Master, if you can, please tell
   about these clashing souls. Were they all priests,
   the tonsured ones who circle on our left?"
And he replied: "In their first life, these men   40
   were so short-sighted they never opened up
   or closed a purse when it was provident.
Their barking voices reenact those lives
   as they face off and try to interrupt
   the accusations of the other side.   45
The ones who have no hair to thatch their heads
   were village priests or cardinals or popes
   whose tonsures topped excessive avarice."
I answered: "With or without their hair, I hoped
   I'd recognize some of these misanthropes   50
   who spat their money out or held it in."
And he replied, "You hoped in vain as their
   vain, squalid hopes have turned to dust which blurs
   their features, hiding who they were from us.
They will butt heads forever, tonsured or not,   55
   rising, resurgent, out of their sepulchers
   to grab the air with closed or open fists.
Bad blood, too thick or thin, has robbed them of
   that bright, fair world and kept them circling round . . .
   I will not waste more words on this affair.   60
Now see, my son, how Fortune plays a joke:
   her sovereignty of earthly goods compounds
   men's interest; so they brawl and swindle;
Not all the gold that is or ever was
   beneath the moon, below fair heaven's tent   65
   could satisfy one of these weary souls."

"Master," I said to him, "please tell me more
    about her—Fortune—whom you just now mentioned.
    Why does she keep the world's goods clutched so close?"
"What foolish creatures all men are, so full   70
    of ignorance, however well-intentioned!
    I will explain; please take in what I say.
The wisest One, whose wisdom transcends all,
    created the heavens, and gave to each an angel/
    sage; each sphere illumines every other   75
With brightness that diffuses equally.
    So, in the earthly sphere He picked, as well,
    an angel/sage, to rule all splendors. She
Assesses the world's goods, those empty prizes,
    and, smiling at men's reasoning, she decides   80
    which state or family will get the spoils.
So one state rules, another languishes,
    pursuant to her judgment's law, which hides,
    a snake uncoiled and waiting in the grass.
Your wisdom cannot influence her rule;   85
    she foresees, takes control, pursues her wishes,
    as do all other gods within their spheres.
Her shifts and changes can't be overturned;
    with speed that makes her words seem gibberish,
    she gives and in an instant takes away.   90
How often she is vilified and damned
    even by those whose riches she has spawned,
    as if good Fortune's fortune is a curse.
But she is blest—beatitude is deaf—
    and, joining the other creatures God made at dawn,   95
    she spins her sphere and glories in her bliss.
But now let us descend to greater misery;
    the stars that rose above when we set out
    have set; we're not allowed to slow our pace."
We crossed the circle to the other bank   100
    and walked beside a boiling waterspout
    which carved a channel for its own escape.

The water was darker there than deepest blue,
   and we, along with waves more gray than white,
   moved down the path, a rough, unfathomable flume   105
Through which the stream of sadness, Styx, descends
   into the marsh named after it. Despite
   our journey down that gray and evil slope,
My eyes, gazing intently at the marsh
   were not prepared . . . the people—such a sight—   110
   waist-deep in mud, naked and furious.
They struck each other, not only with their hands,
   but with their heads and chests, and with their feet;
   their teeth sank in each other's tender flesh.
"Now, son, you see," my gentle master said,   115
   "the souls of those whom anger has defeated;
   and I would have you know for certain that
Beneath the water there are people who
   exhale such sighs they fill the pond with froth.
   See, the water bubbles with their breath.   120
Trapped in the slime, they say: 'Once we were sullen
   and we inhaled the smoke of our own sloth
   even in air both sweet and drenched with sun;
So now we are bogged down in this black mire.'
   This is the hymn they snuffle out like shoats   125
   because they cannot sing it out in words."
And so we walked and talked, past the pond of bloat,
   between the dry bank and the bursting shower,
   our eyes on those with mud stuffed down their throats.
Eventually we came upon a tower.   130

CANTO VIII / *Cynthia Macdonald*

To carry on from there: before we reached
   the foot of that high tower, we surveyed
   its length, and fixed our eyes upon the top
Where two small flames, two signal flames
   were set. Another flame, so far away   5
   the eye could hardly see it, signaled back.
And I turned to the font of wisdom: "Who
   has set these flares? And why? What messages
   do they transmit, these two and that dim one?"
And he: "The marshy mist almost conceals   10
   what has been summoned here. Through those passages
   of filthy troughs and crests, it rides the waves."
No arrow ever hurtled from a bow—
   sent aloft as if to puncture the air—
   with greater speed than that boat sped toward us,   15
Skimming the water straight to where we stood;
   it held a single boatman who declared,
   his face alight, "I've got you, arrogant soul."
"Phlegyas, Phlegyas, this time you waste your breath,"
   my master said. "You'll have us in your grasp   20
   no longer than it takes to cross the marsh."
As one who has been tricked by some deceit
   puffs up with anger and is filled with wrath,
   so Phlegyas did, deprived of us, his prey.
My leader stepped into the boat which did   25
   not rock or move, although it seemed to founder
   when I got in, as if my weight would sink it.
As soon as he and I were both on board
   the boat moved off with far more roil and stir
   than when it carried only spirit cargo.   30

And as the ancient prow moved through the channel,
  a fecal shape rose from the marshy flood
  and spoke: "Who is it—come before his time?"
I answered: "I have come, but won't remain.
  But you—who are you, so disguised by mud?"   35
  He said, "You see that I am one who weeps."
And I replied, "With all your tears and grief,
  malignant soul—it's right that you are here;
  I know you even though you're caked with filth."
The shape stretched out his hands to grab the boat,   40
  but no, my master quickly interfered,
  "Stay where you are, with all the other dogs."
Then putting both his arms around my neck,
  he kissed me on the cheek, "Indignant soul,
  blest is the one who bore you in her womb.   45
In life, this man was arrogant and cruel;
  there's not one stroke of virtue on the scroll
  which lists his deeds; so now he's mad with rage.
Many, who in the world are puffed-up tyrants,
  leaving behind them only disrepute,   50
  down here will wallow in the muck like pigs."
And then I said, "I can't conceive more pleasure
  than seeing him sopped down in this thick stew
  before we land and leave the lake behind."
"Your wish will be fulfilled," my master said,   55
  "before the border of the far shore comes in view
  he will be set upon—your just reward."
And shortly afterward he was the target
  of such fierce rending by the muddy horde
  that even now I still give thanks to God.   60
"Let's get Filippo Argenti," they cried out.
  That Florentine, with Florentine discord,
  attacked his angry flesh with his own teeth.
We left him there; I've told more than enough.
  But now the saddest wailing filled my ears;   65
  I strained my eyes to see what I could see.

My gentle master said, "See here, my son,
   the city known as Dis will soon appear,
   with its grave citizens, its vast battalions."
"Master, already I can see its mosques   70
   emerging from the valley just ahead,
   vermillion, as if they flower from a flame."
And he to me: "It is the eternal flame
   which lights them from inside and turns them red.
   This sight means we have come to deeper Hell."   75
We went into the bedrock moats which bound
   this walled disconsolate city, circling walls
   which seemed, I thought, to be forged out of iron.
We had to circle virtually the whole moat
   to reach the spot where the boatman harshly called,   80
   "Get out; you'll find the entrance over there."
Above the gates I saw a multitude
   of creatures who in heaven were once divine.
   They cried, "Who are you who, without being dead,
Dare come into this kingdom of the dead?"   85
   My master knew that he must make a sign
   to show he wished to talk to them in secret.
He did; they slightly lessened their disdain
   and said, "You stay, but let him go, that one
   who dared to enter here and breach our realm.   90
He'll have to circle back on the fool's journey
   which he chose; yes, let him go alone
   without an escort; you must stay with us."
Imagine, reader, my discomfort when
   I heard the sound of those appalling words.   95
   I thought I'd never get back to this world.
"O dearest guide, who more than seven times
   restored my spirit, you who always heard
   my fears and kept me safe when danger loomed,
Do not desert me when I need you most.   100
   And if we can't go on together, let's
   retrace our steps as quickly as we can."

That lord who'd guided me thus far replied,
  "Don't be afraid, for those on high attest
  our right to passage; we cannot be stopped.   105
Wait here for me and rest, and let your weary
  spirit feed on comfort and sweet hope.
  I won't desert you in this underworld."
Away he goes, abandons me right there,
  that gentle father, leaving me to cope   110
  with "yes" and "no" resounding in my head.
I could not hear what he proposed to them,
  but they turned tail and scrambled back inside
  the walls before much time had passed.
They slammed the gates, those adversaries of ours,   115
  right in my teacher's face; he stood outside,
  then with slow steps he turned to me again.
His eyes were on the ground, his forehead creased,
  all boldness wiped away; he sighed, "Who are
  they to exclude me from the house of grief!"   120
And then to me: "You need not be dismayed
  because I am perturbed, for we have far
  to go and shall; no one can block our way.
This insolence of theirs is nothing new;
  they used it once before to try and bar   125
  the gate which Christ passed through; it's still unbarred.
Above it in the stone, cut like a scar,
  are those dead words: 'Abandon hope all ye . . .'
  Already past that gate, almost to where we are
Comes one who'll unlock Dis without a key."   130

CANTO IX / *Amy Clampitt*

Seeing me stand there green with fear, my guide,
    returning, the more quickly bottled up
    the look that told me he was newly worried.
He halted, listening; for through that murk,
    that black air's vaporous density, the eye   5
    could hardly venture. "Surely in the end
We must win out," he said. "If not . . ."
    A pause. "Assurances were given. But so
    much time, and still no sign of anyone!"
I heard too vividly how he dissembled,   10
    overlaying what he had begun
    to say with words that differed so,
I grew more fearful still—more than,
    perhaps, his hesitation warranted,
    inferring from it worse than what he'd meant.   15
"Does anyone," I asked him then, "go deep
    as this, into this godforsaken hollow,
    from that level where the sole penalty
Is hope cut off?" "Rarely," he answered,
    "does any of us from that first circle   20
    follow the downward track we travel now—
Though I myself once did so, conjured by
    the witch Erichtho, whose power it was
    to mingle shade with corpse again. My own
Remains were not long nude of me before   25
    she summoned me to pass within that wall
    and fetch a shade from the abode of Judas—
A circle farther down and darker, more
    remote from all that's good, than any other.
    Oh, I know the way, you may be certain.   30

This marsh from which so huge a stench goes up
   girdles the doleful metropolis.
   Rage will confront us here before we enter."
What he said next I now forget, my sight
   being drawn by then to what appeared   35
   lit up by the infernal glare within
Those towers: three hellish things that had
   in form and attitude the look of women,
   blood-smeared, greenly garlanded at waist
And temple by a clutch of water snakes,   40
   wildly writhing, serpentine-haired,
   viperish: such were the Furies.
He who well knew these minions from the household
   of her who rules where groaning never ends,
   named for me one by one the foul Erinyes: 45
"That is Megaera to the left; the one
   who ravens on the right, Alecto; and
   between the two, Tisiphone." He halted,
As each clawed or struck with open palm
   at her own person, shrieking so fiendishly   50
   I shuddered, and moved closer to the poet.
"Call for Medusa: she'll turn him to rock,"
   regarding us below, they howled as one.
   "What Theseus tried here is not yet paid back."
"Turn round, and keep your eyes closed. Were   55
   the Gorgon to appear, and you to look,
   all chance of our return would be forgone."
These were the master's words, as his own hands,
   not to rely on mine, enclosed them in
   another, outer band about my forehead.   60
You who are sound of understanding, note,
   I say, what trove of doctrine is concealed
   beneath the seeming strangeness of this passage.
There came now from about the turbid moat
   an uproar such as caused its shores to rumble— 65
   a fracas of confused alarm, as when

A holocaust of torrid gusts, igniting
   without check, engulfs a wilderness,
   whose snapped limbs' scorched and crackling litter,
Pulverized, grown irresistible,   70
   drives the animals and those who herd them,
   gasping and terrified, alike before it.
Uncovering my eyes, my guide said, "Look
   now across that antiquated scum,
   to just where the fumes are deadliest."   75
As frogs, when the predatory snake
   pursues them, vanish, plunging headlong
   into the muck, and squat there, hiding,
Ruined souls, more than a thousand of them,
   I saw in flight from one who, moving dry   80
   of foot above the Styx, passed swiftly over.
Repeatedly his left hand fanned away
   the rank air from before him—the one
   sign he gave at all of being vexed.
Well aware of where this being came from,   85
   it was my guide I turned to now, and at
   a sign from him, I offered mute obeisance.
Ah, how terrible in indignation
   that one appeared! He held a little rod.
   I saw the gate give way, without resistance.   90
I saw him stand there on the horrid threshold.
   "O you despised and outcast ones," he cried,
   "why do you harbor such excessive rage?
Why such recalcitrance toward that Will
   whose purposes endure unmoved forever,   95
   whom to resist adds to your suffering?
What use to butt against what is ordained?
   Your watchdog Cerberus still bears those scars
   about the neck that are the proof of this."
To the foul thoroughfare he now returned   100
   without a word for us, but with the look
   of one who's spurred on by a care beyond

What human thought could possibly encompass.
    We moved our steps to pass within, secure
    now the angelic words had been pronounced,   105
And entered without raising any outcry.
    Then I, desiring eagerly to learn
    the state of those confined in that grim fortress,
Cast wondering eyes about me. What I saw
    was a vast, open desert place, the haunt   110
    of ire and the most dreadful torment.
As where, at Arles, the Rhône goes stagnant, or
    in the low-lying precincts of Quarnaro,
    past the Italian boundary at Pola,
The burial mounds that crowd those graveyards make,   115
    on every side, a rough terrain: thus was
    it here, but far more grievously:
Among the mounds the soil was all afire,
    so fervently, each tomb appeared to glare
    hotter than any smelter's craft has need for.   120
Each lid was up, and from below it came
    the groans of one within, whose misery,
    thus heard, seemed hardly bearable.
"Master," I said then, "what people lie
    casketed within those sepulchers,   125
    lamenting without end the end they've come to?"
And he: "Here lie the greatest heretics
    of every sect, with all their followers.
    More of them than you would suppose are thus
Interred, like next to like, in monuments   130
    of varying degrees of burning." Turning
    to the right, we passed between those torments
And the high walls that encircled them.

CANTO X / *Amy Clampitt*

Along a secret track between the ramparts
   and those sufferings we made our way.
   From close upon the shoulder of the one
Who led I asked, "O sum of virtue, guide
   through the unholy gyres, whose lead I follow,   5
   tell me, if you will—I burn to know—
Whether possibly, of those who lie there,
   we might see any? All the tombs appear
   to be uncovered, and no one guards them."
"Each one will be shut up again," he said,   10
   "when from the valley of Jehoshaphat
   the dead are gathered for the final judgment.
At present, Epicurus and all who
   asserted that the soul dies with the body
   are assigned to lie here. Shortly,   15
From in there, what you have asked me
   will be answered, and also that other
   curiosity which goes unvoiced."
And I said: "Dear guide, I would withhold
   nothing from you, but that to speak little   20
   is the way your caution has inclined me."
"O Tuscan"—suddenly a voice rang from
   its lodging place—"you who alive traverse
   this burning plain, whose speech is decorous,
Might you, if you will, be good enough   25
   to pause here and address me? From that tongue
   I know your noble birthplace, toward which
I acted once, perhaps, with undue harshness."
   On hearing this, being shaken once again,
   I drew close to the one who owned my trust.   30

"Turn round," he directed. "What's the matter?
   Look: there, so erect, stands Farinata.
   You may, from the waist up, now see him clearly."
My gaze already had been fixed by his.
   Chest outthrust, head high, it was as though   35
   he looked with grand contempt on hell itself.
My guide's hands then, quickly and forcibly,
   propelled me through the field of sepulchers
   to meet that other, saying, "Mind how you speak."
I made my way toward the tomb's foot, where   40
   he stared a moment, then asked, in some
   disdain, "Of whom are *you* descended?"
With no unwillingness I answered, leaving
   nothing out; and he with lifted eyebrow,
   condescending even in the pit,   45
Declared: "They were to my forebears and me
   ferociously opposed; I and my party
   not once but twice dispersed them totally."
"Scattered though they may have been, they learned
   not once but twice," I said, "how to come back—   50
   an art your faction never did acquire."
Beside him, at that moment, another shade
   emerged that must—since what I saw was from
   chin upward only—have risen to its knees,
And seemed to peer about me as though driven   55
   by a hope some other might be with me.
   Then, disappointed, he addressed me
Weeping: "If genius of a high degree
   brings you to this blind hole, where is
   my son, then? Why is he not with you?"   60
"That I come here," I said, "is not my doing.
   The one who stands there leads me on this journey,
   one whom it would seem your Guido scoffed at."
His query, and the form his punishment
   had taken, told me unmistakably   65
   the name the shade had borne; hence my response.

Pulling himself erect, he cried, "Why 'scoffed'?
  Is he not still among the living? Do
  his eyes not drink, still, the delicious day?"
Finding me unready to reply,   70
  the shade whose son had been my intimate
  fell back. That was the last I saw of him.
Meanwhile the face of that stiff-natured one
  at whose behest I stood there changed not at all,
  nor did his head turn, nor his body bend,   75
As he took up our colloquy: "If they
  have failed at that," he said, "the thought disturbs me
  far more than any torment of this bed.
That queen whose phases govern here shall not
  have fifty times grown round again before   80
  you in your turn shall know how hard it is.
And that you may to the sweet world up there
  go safely back, tell why in all their laws
  your party are so fierce against my kin?"
To this I said: "The bloody rout that turned   85
  the Arbia to crimson cannot but
  invoke in patriots a late revenge."
His breathing tightened, and his head wagged. "In
  all that," he said, "I did not act alone,
  and surely others were not without cause.   90
But when the rallying cry was 'Down with Florence!
  Raze every bell tower!' it was I who rose
  to argue openly against such rashness."
"That your descendants may one day know peace,"
  I said, "I beg you to undo for me   95
  the knot that now impedes my comprehension.
If I have heard correctly, it would seem
  that what is still to come you may discern,
  yet with the present it is otherwise."
He said, "We see as those whose vision blurs   100
  what's near at hand, whereas things at a distance
  grow clear: such sovereign light is granted us.

Concerning present scenes we speculate
   in vain: except when others bring us word
   of your affairs, we down here know nothing.   105
You see how, with the future's threshold crossed,
   and the door shut on what was yet to come,
   from that point all our knowledge perishes."
I said then with compunction, "Will you, sir,
   inform him who just now slid back beside you   110
   his son is still indeed among the living—
And that my failure to respond before
   was owing to my own bewilderment
   concerning matters you have since made clear."
My guide now having summoned me to join him,   115
   it was the more in haste I begged the shade
   to name for me what others were there with him.
He said, "There are here more than a thousand.
   The second Frederick is one, the Cardinal
   another. Of the rest I do not speak."   120
With that he disappeared. I turned then, still
   preoccupied with all the enmity
   in what I'd heard, to join the poet I revered.
He moved on and, as we proceeded,
   asked, "What is it that so troubles you?"   125
   Sagely, when I had told him, he enjoined me:
"Bear those things well in mind which have been said
   to your disfavor. Meanwhile"—with a gesture—
   "pay careful heed to all that you see here.
Once you achieve the dulcet company   130
   of her whose clear eyes miss nothing, all
   you have need to know will be disclosed."
His steps veered now toward the center, leftward;
   leaving the wall, we entered on a trail
   down to a ravine from which there issued   135
Stinks that already brought on nausea.

CANTO XI / *Jorie Graham*

Then on the upper rim of a deep ravine—
a circular ledge of shattered rocks—
we came upon an even crueler drop

and here, given the horrible rising stench
the hole spit forth, took cover   5
behind the fallen lid of an imposing vault.

On it I saw some words inscribed—
"Pope Anastasius I now own
whom Fontin tempted from the righteous path."

"Let us postpone descending for a while"   10
—the Master said—"that you grow used
to the sad stench. After a short while

human senses numb. . . ."
To which I ventured, "May we at least then
use this time—that it not simply register as   15

lost?" "You've read my mind," he said, "my
son. Within these broken stones, these cliffs,
three interlocking shrinking spheres descend,

three rings, like this one we now leave—and all
are full of spirits cursed and damned.   20
That, later on, the sight of them—the memory of that

sight—suffice and satisfy your mind,
let me explain, that you may understand,
why it is that they are so confined.

Every wickedness that earns the hatred of   25
the skies involves Injustice. And each
injustice born of fraud, or misused twisted will,
                                        spills over

like a stain from soul to soul.
And as deceit—of all the sins—remains the one most wholly,
most uniquely, man's, it most arouses the God's   30

ire. Therefore the liars are at the bottom of the pit.
Therefore most pain assails them. . . .
You see, the whole of the first circle holds the violent,

but because violence always sears three persons,
the circle splits and spills and builds again into three rings.   35
Violence is done to God. Violence is done to one's

own self. And finally, most literally, to one's own
                                        neighbor is
the violence done. . . . Let me explain.
Upon your brother, upon his being and upon

his property, death and ruin may be   40
wrought. Burnings. Extortions. Devastations.
Therefore the first ring holds the homicides

and everyone who wounds by greed
—pillaging, plundering—all of these souls
in various gathered groups now, drifting.   45

A man or woman may lay violent hand upon
                              themselves,
upon their person, or their property,
and so, here in the second ring, each one who has deprived
                                        himself

—by violence or by violent self-destructive disregard,
                              by dissipation—
of your world, your flesh—he who has wept   50
there where he should be joyous—

here in the second circle must and will
repeatedly repent in vain . . .

But against God violence also may be done.
Denying God, barring God access to your heart,   55
ignoring Nature, ignoring Nature's power, beauty or
                              truthfulness.

Therefore look down and see—further in yet—the lower ring
and how it seethes with Sodomites and usurers and all
                              the rest
who secretly speak inwardly against the evidence
                    of God.

Finally, upon the one who trusts in him, upon
                    a friend,   60
as too upon a total stranger—even an enemy—a man
                    may practice
fraud. It stings. A wound upon conscience.

And though upon a stranger fraud breaks the natural bond
of human love (what we call *nature*)—(and you can see
here in the second ring how all these   65

hypocrites and flatterers and sorcerers and
thieves and panderers have made
their filthy nest)—the trust placed in a *friend*,

broken, breaks both that natural bond
and the created one—the personal, most crucial bond—So that
                          it's in   70
the smallest, narrowest, darkest spot

at the center of the Universe
that every traitor is consumed, eternally.
Those fires will never cease to burn."

And then I asked him, "Master, your speech   75
clearly describes this chasm and the souls it holds,
but those souls in the bog, down there,

and them whom the wind drives, and them whom the rain
devours, and those down there who scream and curse—that
                            bitterness
I hear—why aren't they punished too in this metropolis of
                          blood and fire?   80

Or is God's anger not upon them?
And if it isn't, why
do they suffer so?" And he to me,

"Why do your thoughts wander from their
                      rightful
course? Where else is your mind   85
wandering? What do you see?
Don't you recall the words with which the
                    Ethics names

what God's will most abhors:
incontinence, malice, and *mad bestiality*—
and how incontinence offends, but is not damned as
       mightily?   90
Think, therefore, consider and imagine,

who those are that suffer punishment up there—
Can't you see clearly why they're separated from
those other acid souls, why the God's vengeance
hammers them less spitefully?"   95

"Master, you heal as sunlight would
   my troubled vision.
You make the questioning more valuable
—by your response—than having known, or
     knowing. But please

go back to where you said how usury
offends the God. Free that knot up
     for me."   100
That's when he said, "For one who's listening,

Philosophy, at every turn, points out
how nature takes her shape from the God's Intellect.
From His Imagination. So in the *Physics* you will find

that Poetry (as far as it can do)   105
also must follow Nature's swift
command—this Art of yours,

therefore, almost a grand-child of the God, a great
      grand-child . . .
Because Man must (remember Genesis)
turn to these two—Nature and God—to make   110

his life, to prosper, reap, to send forth men
upon the earth. . . . The usurer—
because he goes the other way—contradicts Nature

both in her body and her soul
by trying to hoard and then to squander her.   115
It seems he would extinguish her rather than spend

her gifts . . . But follow me,

for now it pleases me to go,

the patterns of the stars are quivering
                    near the horizon now,   120
the north wind's picking up, and farther on
there is the cliff's edge we must reach

to start down from . . ."

CANTO XII / *Jorie Graham*

The way down was steep and mountainous.
And at the bottom of the drop, spread out before us,
were sights that any human eye would shun.

For not unlike where the deadly quake (whether by
sheer strength of tremor, or merely lack of   5
underpinning structure—I couldn't say) ravaged the Adige

clear up to Trent—whole mountains ripped down
into the plain—so here the whole facade of the ravine
was crushed and wrecked, making descent

near unimaginable. And on the rim, above the scree,   10
reclining, horribly calm, we saw a beast—the offspring of
Crete's mythic pagan cow—staring at us,

and as it stared, it bent its head down to its chest
and bit itself—rage crumpling its body inward
over its soul. My wise man called to it—   15

"You seem to think this one the Duke of Athens,
who in the upper world dealt you your mortal blow—
Away with you, creature! This man

not by your sister's guile—or any other mortal's will—
but by some other hand has found   20
his way to you, a witness to your pain."

[52]

With that—just as a bull, receiving suddenly his mortal blow,
snaps loose, and knows not where to turn
but, hopping, plunging, twists back and forth and here and there—

the minotaur now broke and swung. "Run," my guide cried out—   25
"while he is venting you can slip by—and then descend—it's well—
                                                    go now."

So over scree and rock that gave way underfoot—
as if stunned by my human weight—
we made our way. Me lost in

thought. And him (sudden, as always): "You contemplate perhaps   30
this devastation? this beast whose rage

was quenched just now by words?
The only other time I came down here—into this
                              nether Hell—
none of the rock had crumbled yet,

although it wasn't long (if I have read it right)   35
before He came who carried off from here
the Great Ones of the upper rim—

such a great spoil it rocked this
                  deep foul valley
on all sides until I thought
the universe *felt love*, or felt that love   40

which has often before in time turned
that which we call the world to its chaotic
inverse—inside out—

and in that instant, in that passage, this rock—
here, but not only here—felt such a turning of the universal   45
gears—backwards—backwards . . .

But look down now and pay attention.
The river of our blood draws near.
And in the blood, those who in life hurt others
                              violently,

erupt and boil. O blind cupidity   50
and rage, who in our tiny life
so goad us on, madly, and then, in this
                              eternity

drown us so deep in our own bitterness and
                    misery . . ."
Before me suddenly a draw arced open round,
as if to hold within itself the view in its
                              entirety   55

(just as my escort said it would) and in it,
centaurs were running, armed with bows,
in single file, as when in life they hunted, free—

Seeing us come they stopped. Three, choosing their
arrows, moved on us.   60
One, from a little distance, cried

"What martyrdom is it you seek
you who descend? Speak up. Do not
approach. Speak or I draw my bow—"

To which my guide replied: "We'll speak   65
only to Chiron, there, beside you—
(your overhasty will still governs you)—"

then touched me, whispering, "That one is Nessus—
he died for the beautiful Deianira,
avenging himself upon himself—   70

and the one in the middle, standing now,
Chiron, Achilles' tutor—
and the other one, the one so full of rage, Pholus—

around this ditch they go, thousands of their
                                    arrows
piercing any soul who dares rise up out of the stream
                                    of blood   75
more than its guilt and sentencing allows."

We drew closer to them, agile swift beasts.
Chiron—using an arrow from his pack—
tucked back his beard till we could see his great mouth

gleam. To his companions said: 80
"Have you seen how the one behind
moves everything he walks upon?—

that is not how the dead men's feet proceed . . ."
And my leader, having reached the Satyr's side—
                                    his breast—
there where his two worlds are conjoined and
                                    flow   85

into each other—said,
"Yes, he is alive. The only one. My task
to show him through the dark.
Necessity compels him, not curiosity.

She who assigned me to this task,   90
who from her grace and choiring briefly drew aside to send me
                                    here, guarantees
he is no thief. Nor I one of the thieving shades.

Therefore, by that power, that unsurpassable virtue
which set me in motion, step by step, along this
                    bloody path,
supply us with one of your herd,   95

one who can show us where safe crossing is,
and who can take this man, whose weight
the air can't lift, upon his back."

Chiron swirled round to Nessus.
"Go back and escort them. If other herds   100
approach or threaten you, make them give way."

So we set off with trusted guide,
first 'long the rim, then at the very froth-edge of
                    the boiling blood
from which the victims' shrieking rose . . .

And it was then I saw them—souls submerged in blood
                            up to their eyes . . .   105
"Tyrants"—the great centaur called out to me—
"The ones who dealt in flesh and blood and spoils

and plunder. See how they mourn
their ruthless crimes—Alexander, merciless
                    Dionysius
whom the Sicilians learned to hate—and that black   110

shock of hair, down there, is Azzolino,
and that blond head, Obizzo d'Este, who up in
                    your world
met death from his own offspring's

hand"—(I turned to Virgil but he admonished—
"*listen* to him, he is your guide for now")—   115
then turning back found the great beast just slowing down beside
                    a crowd

whose heads and necks emerged from the hot frothing stream
and (as he pointed to a shade off to the side, alone)
heard him spit forth, (but soft): "That one stole from

God's very lap the heart whose blood still stains   120
the Thames." Then I saw some who stood
only waist-deep in blood. And among these

so many that I knew . . .
Thus gradually the blood sank down,
till finally the damned stood only ankle-deep in it   125

—only their feet on fire with blood—and here
our narrow pass out of the steaming ditch appeared.
"Though this stream thins here," motioned our guide,

"it is important that you know how on the other
                                        side
it deepens once again, and flows round, deepening,
                                        always deepening,   130
till it rejoins that bottomless dark pool again

where Tyranny, drowned and blinded, groans—
Attila—whose evil spread like a disease—
and Pyrrhus, and Sextus, and all whom divine Justice now can

sting repeatedly—thick stream whose fires   135
forever milk the tears from Rinier da Corneto,
from Rinier Pazzo—from all who terrorized and terrorize

those who would venture forth, those who would trust
                                        the open road. . . ."
Then he turned quickly from us
and slipped back through the narrow pass.   140

Nessus had not yet arrived at the other side
   when we began to make our way through a wood
   unmarked or blazed by any kind of path.
Not one green leaf on any tree, just black;
   no smooth, straight limbs, just gnarled ones, warped and knotted;   5
   no fruit was on them, just poisoned twigs and thorns.
Wild beasts that hate the cultivated land
   from Cecina to Cornetto don't have such harsh
   and twisted thickets as these to hide away in.
For here the brutish Harpies make their nests,   10
   who flushed the Trojans from the Strophades
   with sad announcement of their future harm.
They have wide wings, and human necks and faces,
   clawed feet, great bellies downed and slick with feathers;
   on top of these strange trees, they keen and lament.   15
My good master said, "Before you go farther in,
   remember that you are in the second ring,
   and will be," he continued on, "until
You reach the edge of the terrifying sand.
   Therefore, look sharply, you are going to see   20
   such things you wouldn't believe from my mere mouth."
From every side I heard the drawn-out wails,
   but saw no person there who might have made them,
   so stopped, therefore, in true bewilderment,
Believing he believed that I believed   25
   that all those voices came, among the trunks,
   from people who were hidden away from us.
Whereupon the master said, "If you break off
   a little branch from any one of these plants,
   the thoughts you have will also be broken off."   30

So I stretched out my hand a little way,
   and broke, from a great thornbush, a small twig;
   its branch cried out, "Why have you broken me?"
Afterward, when its wound had darkened with blood,
   it began again: "Why did you tear that off?   35
   Have you no compassion whatsoever, no pity?
We were men once, and now we are underbrush:
   surely your hand would have been more merciful
   even if we had been the souls of snakes."
Like a green log that smolders at one end   40
   and from the other drips and hisses sap
   forced out and audibled by the burned air,
So from the splintered branch together oozed
   both words and blood; I let the twig-end drop
   and stood stock-still, like one who is afraid.   45
"If he had been able to believe before,
   wounded spirit," my sage replied to him,
   "what he had only seen once in my poem,
He never would have raised his hand against you;
   but so incredible a thing enticed me   50
   to urge him to a deed that grieves me now.
But tell him who you were, so he can make
   amends, and can refresh your fame above
   in the world where he is destined to return."
And the branch said: "Your sweet words allure me so   55
   I can't keep silent; may it not burden you
   if I am lured to talk a little while.
I am the one who held fast to both the keys
   of Frederick's heart, who turned them with such finesse,
   both locking and unlocking, that every one   60
Was kept outside his secrets but myself;
   I was so faithful to that glorious office,
   that for it in time I lost both sleep and life.
The whore who never turned her sluttish eyes
   away from Caesar's household and retinue,   65
   the common death and common vice of courts,

Inflamed the hearts and minds of all against me;
   then those enflamed did so enflame Augustus
   my happy honors soon changed to sad laments.
My mind, in its disdainful temperament, 70
   thinking by dying to escape disdain,
   made me unjust against my own just self.
By the new roots of this tree I have become,
   I swear to you that I never broke the faith
   with my lord, who was so worthy and honorable. 75
If either of you returns up to the world,
   comfort my memory, my fame that lies
   still prostrate from the blow that envy gave it."
He waited a little, and then, "Since he is silent,"
   the poet said to me, "don't hesitate, 80
   but speak, and ask him what you want to know."
To which I answered, "Ask him yourself again
   whatever you think that I might ask myself,
   for I cannot, such pity mutes my heart."
Therefore he started over, "So that this man, 85
   imprisoned spirit, may freely do for you
   what you have asked, please tell us more of how
The soul becomes bound up in these fierce knots,
   and tell us, if you can, if any soul
   is ever loosened from his limbs and freed." 90
The branch puffed hard to clear itself, and soon
   that wind had turned itself into a voice:
   "Briefly I'll answer you, and what you ask.
When the ferocious soul uproots itself
   and quits the body that had sheltered it, 95
   Minos deploys it to the seventh throat.
It falls into the woods, and no one part
   is chosen; but wherever fortune flings it
   there it germinates like a grain of wheat.
Then shoots up like a sapling, a wild growth: 100
   the Harpies, grazing later upon its leaves,
   give pain, and give an outlet to the pain.

Like all the others, we shall return to claim
    our flesh, but unlike them shall never wear it—
    it is not just to have what you've forsaken.   105
Here shall we drag it, and through the mournful wood
    our bodies shall be hung, each on a thorn,
    each on the thornbush of its violent shade."
We were attentive still upon the branch,
    believing that it might have more to tell us,   110
    when we were surprised and diverted by a roar,
Such as the hunter hears when he keeps his stand,
    hearing the wild boar and the chase itself,
    hearing the beasts approach, and the branches crack.
And here were two of them off to the left,   115
    naked and terribly torn, fleeing so hard
    they broke each tree branch that they hurtled through.
The one in front: "Come on, Death, now come on!"
    The other, thinking he couldn't keep up the pace,
    was screaming, "Lano, your legs were not so nimble   120
Jousting and running away along the Toppo!"
    Then, maybe because his breath was failing him,
    he fell and became one tangle with a bush.
Behind their backs, the wood was growing full
    of black she-dogs, as eager and as swift   125
    as greyhounds just unfastened from their chains.
They sank their teeth in the one who had squatted down,
    and then they tore him apart, piece by piece,
    then carried away the shredded, miserable limbs.
At this my escort took me by the hand   130
    and led me to the bush whose crying voice
    issued in vain through its broken and bleeding wounds.
"O Jacopo da Santo Andrea," it said,
    "what have you gained by making a screen of me?
    What blame have I for your past sinful life?"   135
When my master had stopped and was standing over it,
    he said, "Who were you who through so many wounds
    breathes with your blood your melancholy words?"

And he to us: "O souls who have arrived
    in time to see such immoral mutilation,   140
    that stripped my leaves and left my branches torn,
Gather them at the foot of this wretched bush.
    I was of the city which changed her patronage
    from Mars to John the Baptist, for which reason
His art will always make her sorrowful;   145
    and were it not that on the Arno's bridge
    some semblance of his image still remains,
Those citizens who afterward rebuilt
    on top of the ashes that Attila left,
    would surely have done their labors all in vain.   150
Out of my house I made my hanging tree."

CANTO XIV / *Charles Wright*

Because the love I had for my native place
   moved me, I gathered up the scattered leaves
   and gave them back to him, his voice now faint.
From there we came to the boundary line that divides
   the second ring from the third, and where we saw   5
   the terrifying justice of God's hand.
To make come clear things never seen before,
   I tell you we came upon an open plain
   where nothing grew, and nothing made its bed.
The sorrowful wood is garlanded around it,   10
   as the wood itself is wound by the river of blood;
   we stopped here, the very edge, the border line.
The ground was made of sand, compact and dry,
   a sand no different in its kind and makeup
   from that which Cato in his death march trod.   15
O vengeance of God, how just that you should be
   dreaded by everyone whose eyes can read
   what now has been revealed to my own eyes!
I witnessed many herds of naked souls
   lamenting and weeping miserably, and it seemed   20
   that different laws had been imposed upon them.
Flat on their backs, some lay upon the ground,
   others were huddled together in a crouch,
   and some were moving incessantly around.
Those milling about were far more numerous,   25
   and those who were lying on the sand were least,
   but louder in their torment to tongue their pain.
Over the sand, in a kind of slow free-fall,
   huge lumps of fire were swinging silently down,
   like snowflakes that fall in the mountains without wind.   30

Or like the flames that Alexander saw
  in the hot parts of India that fell
  unbroken over his troops and hit the ground;
Who had the entire army tramp down the soil
  and burning pieces before they joined together,   35
  extinguishing them before they began to spread:
Thus did the heat and endless fire descend,
  the sand rekindled by each flame, as flint
  will kindle tinder, redoubling the pain.
The dance, with its jumps and flicks, of wretched hands   40
  went on unceasingly, now here, now there,
  as they tried to brush away the fresh flaked flames.
I started: "Master, you who overcome
  all things except for those unyielding demons
  who set upon us at the entrance gate,   45
Who is that giant who doesn't seem to mind
  the fire, who lies disdainful there and scowls
  as though the rain will never humble him?"
And he himself, who had perceived that I
  was asking about him from my leader, cried: 50
  "That which I was in life, I am in death.
Though Jove wear out his blacksmith from whose forge
  he took in anger the sharp-edged lightning bolt
  which on my last day he thundered down on me;
Or if he wears out the others, one by one,   55
  in Mongibello, at that soot-stained workshop,
  crying out, 'Good Vulcan, help me, help,'
The way he did when there was war at Phlegra,
  and arrow his bolts at me with all his might,
  not even then would he have glad vengeance on me."   60
Then my leader spoke back at him with a force
  I had not ever heard him use before.
  "O Capaneus, because your pride remains
Unquenched, you're made to suffer all the more;
  no other torment than your rage itself   65
  could hope to offer pain to match your fury."

Then, with a kinder countenance, he turned
    to me: "That was one of the seven kings
    who besieged Thebes; he held, and seems still to hold,
God in a great disdain, prizing Him little;   70
    but, as I said to him, his disrespect
    glitters like medals on his odious chest.
Now follow me closely here, and watch you don't
    settle your footsteps on the burning sand,
    but keep them always inside the forest line."   75
In silence we came to a place where there spurted out
    from the darkness of the forest a little stream
    whose viscous redness makes me shudder still.
Like the one that issues from the Bulicame
    the prostitutes divide among themselves,   80
    so this one cut its way across the sand.
Its bottom and both its banks were made of stone,
    as were the walkway edges on each side;
    I saw our passageway was down this path.
"In everything I've pointed out to you   85
    since that moment when we entered through the gate
    whose threshold's no longer denied to anyone,
Nothing as yet has been witnessed by your eyes
    as notable as is this present stream
    above which every falling flame is snuffed."   90
These words were spoken by my master, and I
    implored him to bestow on me the food
    for which he had bestowed the appetite.
"In the middle of the ocean there lies a land
    named Crete, which is a wasteland," he said to me,   95
    "under whose king the world was once innocent.
There is a mountain there which was content
    with water and greenery and is called Ida;
    it's now deserted, like a withered thing.
Rhea had chosen it as the faithful cradle   100
    her son required as a better hiding place;
    to conceal his cries, she had her servants shout.

Inside the mountain, the Old Man's statue stands,
    who has his back turned always toward Damietta,
    and looks toward Rome as though into a mirror.   105
His head is fashioned out of the finest gold,
    and purest silver makes up his arms and chest,
    then brass completes him to where his legs begin;
From there on down he is of choicest iron,
    except for the right foot, which is terracotta,   110
    upon which he rests, more than upon the other.
All of the parts are broken, except the gold,
    by a fissure that dribbles tears down to his feet,
    where they collect and cut through the cavern floor.
From rock to rock they gather into this valley,   115
    forming the Phlegethon, Acheron and Styx;
    then they are channeled down this tight canal
Until, there where nothing more can descend,
    they form Cocytus—and what that pool is like
    you'll see yourself, I won't describe it here."   120
And then I asked him: "If the present stream
    has such a source, and flows thus from our world,
    why do we see it only at this border?"
And he to me: "You know this place is round,
    and though the distance you have come is far,   125
    down toward the bottom, always circling left,
You haven't as yet completed all the circle;
    so that, if something new appears to us,
    it shouldn't bring such wonder to your face."
And I again: "Master, where do we find   130
    Lethe and Phlegethon? One you don't mention,
    the other you say is formed by this rain of tears."
"Truly you please me in all your questionings,"
    he answered, "but this boiling blood-red water
    should easily solve one of them that you ask.   135
You will see Lethe, but out of this abyss,
    there where the souls repair to cleanse themselves
    when the sin repented of has been removed."

And then he said: "Now it is time to quit
   the wood; make sure you follow close behind me: 140
   these edges form a path that doesn't burn,
Above them each flake of falling fire is quenched."

Now we walk along a hard embankment
  and the river's vapor arches over us,
  preserving earth and water from the fire.
  The Flemings who live between Wissant and Bruges,
  fearing the tides that rise against them, build   5
  dikes to check the sea; so do the Paduans
  along the Brenta, to save their villages
  and castles from Carinthia's melting snow—
  these banks were like that, though the Builder made
  ramparts neither so massive nor so high.   10
By now we had left the Wood so far behind
  that had I stopped and turned around to look
  I never should have made out where it was,
  when a troop of souls ran up beside the dike,
  peering at us, each one, the way at dusk   15
  men eye one another under a new moon;
  and frowning with the effort to see, just as
  an old tailor squints at his needle's eye.
Scrutinized thus by the whole group of them,
  I was recognized by one who plucked my hem   20
  and cried "How wonderful!" and just as he
  reached out I stared at his scorched face until
  the calcined features could no longer keep
  me from knowing him, and touching his cheek
  I answered: "Ser Brunetto, are you here?"   25
And he: "My son, do not be vexed with me
  if Brunetto Latini, these few moments, turns
  back with you, and lets the rest go on."

"Nothing would please me more," I said to him,
   "and should you wish me to sit here with you,   30
   I will, if it is permitted by my guide."
"O son, were any member of this troop
   to stop, even an instant, he must lie
   a hundred years without shielding himself
   from the fire that strikes him. Therefore walk on,   35
   I'll follow at your hem, and later join
   my comrades lamenting their eternal woes."
I dared not step down from the embankment
   to walk beside him, but kept my head bowed
   like a man walking reverently. He began: 40
"What fate or fortune can it be, my son,
   that brings you to this place before your time?
   And who is he who guides you on your way?"
"Up there, where life shines," I answered him,
   "I strayed into a gorge before my age   45
   was half elapsed. Just yesterday at dawn
   I had emerged, when he appeared to me
   the moment I was turning back again,
   and by this path he leads me home." And he:
"Follow your star and you can never fail   50
   to reach a glorious harbor—knowing this
   while I knew life, and seeing Heaven smile
   on your designs, had I not died so soon,
   I would have succored you in all your work.
   But that ungrateful and malignant race   55
   descended from Fiesole of old,
   still reeking of the mountain and the rock,
   will oppose your benefactions—and for cause!
   Among the bitter sorb-trees, no sweet fig
   should ripen. . . . A people ever known as blind,   60
   as avaricious, envious and proud—
   see that you have nothing to do with them!
   Your fortune holds such honor for you, both
   parties will raven against you, but the grass

grows nowhere near the goat! So let the beasts 65
of Fiesole make fodder of themselves
and keep away from the plant (if any grows
upon their dunghill still) in which survives
the holy seed of Romans who remained
when the place became a nest of wickedness." 70
"Had my prayers been granted," I answered him,
    "you would not yet be banished from the life
men live on earth, for in my mind is fixed
—where it mortifies my heart—your dear, kind,
paternal image when hourly, in the world, 75
you taught me the meaning of eternal life.
As for my gratitude, so long as I live
it is right that I declare it in my speech.
What you tell me of my future I shall write
and keep, with another writing, to be glossed 80
by a lady who, if I reach her, will know how.
This much I want to make distinct to you:
so my conscience be clear, I am prepared
for Fortune as she wills: such augury
is no news to my ears: let Fortune turn 85
her wheel as she will, and the farmer turn his spade. . . ."
My master, walking ahead, gave me a look
    over his right shoulder, and then remarked:
    "He listens well who hears what has been said."
Yet I continue talking with Ser Brunetto, 90
    asking which of his companions are
most noted, most esteemed. And he to me:
    "It is good to know of some; about the rest
silence is the better part—our time
would be too short for so much colloquy. 95
Know that all were clerks, great men of letters,
and of great fame, defiled in the world of men
by the one sin. Priscian is among
that sorry crew, and Francesco d'Accorso as well,
where if you hankered for such wretchedness 100

you might see, too, the man the pope transferred
from Florence to Vicenza, where now lies
the flesh he so abused. I would say more,
but I may not, nor walk farther—over there
I see a new smoke rising from the sand;   105
people are coming with whom I must not be.
Bear in mind my *Trésor*, in it I live on—
I ask no more." He turned back then and seemed
like those who race for the green cloth in the field
at Verona, except that of them he seemed   110
not one who loses, but the one who wins.

CANTO XVI / *Richard Howard*

Now we had come to where we heard the roar
   of water falling into the next circle, like
   the constant humming in a hive of bees,
   when three shades, running, tore themselves away
   from a great company that was passing by   5
   under the insupportable rain of torment.
   As they approached us, each one shouted out:
"You there, stop! We see by the way you dress
   you must be from our fallen city—stop!"
   Ah, fearful were the wounds, half-healed and new,   10
   the flames had inflicted on their flesh—it still
   distresses me to think of it, even now!
My teacher, hearing their clamor, turned back to me
   and said: "Now wait: these deserve your respect,
   and were it not for the rain of fire which is   15
   the nature of this place, I should propose
   it is more fitting that you run toward them."
No sooner had we stopped than they began
   lamenting again, and when they reached us
   all three joined hands and formed a sort of wheel.   20
   As wrestlers, naked and oiled, attempt to find
   a favorable hold before exchanging blows,
   each shade as he circled kept his eyes on mine
   so that his neck and feet turned in opposite ways.
And one began: "If horror of this wilderness   25
   and our burnt and blackened faces make you scorn
   our prayers and ourselves, then let our fame
   move you to tell us who you are and how
   you walk unharmed on mortal feet through hell.
   He whose steps I follow, though he runs flayed   30

[72]

before me, was nobler in rank than you suppose:
grandson of the good Gualdrada, his name
was Guido Guerra, who in his life on earth
achieved great things by sword and strategy.
The one who comes behind me on the sand   35
is Tegghiaio Aldobrandini, whose voice the world
should have heeded. And I, in torment between
these two, was Jacopo Rusticucci, and
my shrewish wife is the reason I am here."
Just then, had I been shielded from the fire,   40
I would have flung myself down there with them
—and this, I think, my guide would have allowed—
but since I should have then been burnt, my fear
vanquished my good will which made me long
to embrace all three of them. And so I said: 45
"Not scorn but sorrow your state inspires in me
—and so deep it will not leave me soon—
when my guide here spoke words by which I guessed
that such men as yourselves might be approaching.
I am of your city, and all my life   50
have heard your honored names and deeds rehearsed,
and with affection spoken them myself.
Leaving the gall behind, I seek the fruit
my master promises, but first I must
go down to the very center." And he replied: 55
"So may your soul for many years direct
your body, and your fame shine after you,
tell us if valor and courtesy abide
within our city as they used to do,
or if they have vanished altogether, for   60
Guglielmo Borsiere, who but a short while
has endured the torment of this company,
greatly distresses us with such report."
"New people newly rich by sudden gains
have spawned, O Florence, such excess and pride   65
in you, that already you must weep for it!"

This I exclaimed with my head held high,
and the three, taking these words for my reply,
looked at each other as men who hear the truth.
"If at other times," they answered me,   70
"you can so readily grant others content,
happy are you to have such powers of speech!
Therefore, if you escape these dismal haunts
and return to see again the lovely stars,
mind that you speak of us to living men   75
when you rejoice to tell them *I was there*."
They broke their wheel then, and as they ran
away their nimble legs seemed more like wings:
an "amen" could not have been said before
they vanished, whereupon my guide walked on,   80
I followed, and we had gone but a short way
when the sound of water was so close at hand
we scarcely could have heard each other speak.
Just as that river which first holds its course
from Mount Viso eastward, on the left slope   85
of the Appenines—known as the Acquachet above
Forlí, where it loses that name just before
it descends to its low bed down on the plain—
roars there above San Benedetto dell'Alpe
in but one torrent where there might have been   90
a thousand; thus, down one rocky slope
we found those blood-red waters echoing
so loud that soon they would have hurt our ears.
I had a cord which I wore round my waist
(once I had supposed I could use it to catch   95
that spotted pard) and as my master bade,
I loosed and passed it to him, knotted and coiled.
Then he, turning to the right, flung it far out
over the brink and into that abyss.
"Surely," I said to myself, "something strange   100
will answer this strange signal which my guide
observes so keenly." What caution men must use

companioned with those who not only see the deed
but have the wit to understand their thoughts!
"Soon," he said, "you will see the thing rise up   105
which I await and you cannot conceive—
soon it will be granted to your sight."
When truth looks like falsehood, it is always best
that a man should speak as little as he can,
for through no fault of his own he will be blamed;   110
but here I must speak, and by the notes of this
my Comedy—so may they be received
with lasting favor—reader, I swear to you
that rising through the thick and murky air
I now beheld a creature swimming toward us   115
—a sight to startle the most steadfast heart!—
moving like a diver who has gone down
to free the anchor caught upon a reef
or some other barrier hidden in the sea,
and stretching his arms out, drawing in his legs,   120
makes his way back up to the surface again. . . .

CANTO XVII / *Stanley Plumly*

"See now the beast that wears the pointed tail,
   traverses mountains, shatters weapons, breaks
   through walls—malodorous, whose sickness fills
The world"; and thus my master spoke to me
   and waved the beast up to the edge ashore   5
   the near deep end of our brimstone causeway;
And thus the creature flew, a parody
   of fraud, and landed with his upper parts
   alone above the bank, his long bony
Tail trailing into the emptiness, his face   10
   innocent of the grotesque of his body,
   sadly gracious versus his serpent's
Heavy trunk, his paw-length arms hairy up
   to the pits, his flanks and scaly back and
   chest tattooed with twining knots and circlets—   15
Neither Tartars nor the Turks could weave such
   tapestry in color and relief, nor
   Arachne at her loom such spider webs.
The way boats often lie half-stranded on
   the shore, part pulled aground, part drift, the way   20
   the beaver plans against his prey among
The lands of the drunken Germans, the beast
   lay squalid at the causeway's stony edge,
   where the black sand simmers like a desert,
His beast's tail twitching like a scorpion's   25
   or great snake's tongue, forked over the void,
   ready to strike at nothing with its venom.
My master said, "At last it's time to pass
   as close to the beast as possible," so
   descending to our right we dropped ten steps   30

Along the brink above the sand and fire
  and finally reached his rest, below which,
  in a desert crouch, some people sat near.
Here my master said to me: "In order
  to know the ring in full you need to talk   35
  with these lost few to see just how they are,
But don't take long—I'll wait here with the beast
  till you return, and negotiate that
  he might offer the broad strength of his back."
So I went alone along the outer   40
  edge of the seventh circle, out to where
  the sad ones squatted with their eyes on fire
With their despondency, rocking back and forth,
  their hands first here, then there, warding off
  the flames sometimes, sometimes the cinders rough   45
Under the sand. They were dogs in summer
  afflicted at the muzzle and the paws
  by gnats and fleas, the gadfly's bitterness.
I saw in their worn fire-lit faces much,
  but no one I knew, only at the neck   50
  of each an enormous and heavy pouch,
Whose intaglio of colors was like
  a coat-of-arms on which their blood-teared eyes
  focused in obsession, almost delight.
And as I went among them, among some   55
  of their grief-illuminating faces,
  on which the fire played tricks, I picked out one
Deep yellow purse with blue depths blazoned with
  a lion's head, and then another red
  as blood with a white goose whiter than whey,   60
And one that had a light blue pregnant sow
  sewn on a field of white, whose wearer asked,
  "Why are you here in this pit? Go on now!
And since you are alive—at least not dead—
  know that my neighbor Vitaliano   65
  has a place saved for him here at my side.

Among these Florentines I'm Paduan—
    they fairly blind me with their whines and shouts:
    'Send on the soldier with the purse of goats!'"
Then he twisted up his mouth, with his tongue   70
    stuck out, like an ox licking at its nose—
    time to get out of here, I thought, and time
To return to him who might be angry
    with an overstay, so I turned my back
    on these weary souls whose sins were heavy.   75
I found my guide already mounted at
    the hind end of the beast. "Courage," he said,
    "climb up in front of me and the attack
Of the tail"—and so in quartan fear as
    deadly as the chill, shaking in front of   80
    shadows, yet shamed as a servant to his
Master, I took heart and settled down on
    the mass of the monster's shoulders, speechless
    but needing to say nevertheless *Hold on*
To me, as if it needed saying, since   85
    my master—as in such other dangers,
    other fears—read my fear in his embrace,
Ordering the beast, "Now, Geryon, fly, but
    keep your circles wide, as this is live
    weight that you carry." Thus like a beached boat   90
Pushed out slowly from the shore, part by part,
    the thing took off until his tail was clear
    enough to work like an eel and help take
The air into his paws. I was afraid
    all over again, as much as Phaeton   95
    when the reins went slack and broke and burned
Across the sky the Milky Way, as much
    as Icarus when he felt the fire-on-wing
    and heard his father shout too late, "Turn back!"
I could see nothing but air on air on   100
    all sides, nothing but warm impossible
    space and the whole of the beast I was on:

That floats and swims and wheels and descends
   slowly as departure, a series of
   departures, into the breath of the rising   105
Wind. And then I heard the sound of the well
   of thunder, right under us, and stretched
   to see how far it was and horrible,
But not so anxious as to fall, for what
   I heard was Hell, which made me hold on   110
   tighter than before, as I was being held.
And then I saw with each slow tightening of
   the circles all that had been hidden—
   the closing-in of fire, the endless crying-out
Of pain. Like a falcon too long in flight   115
   from hunting yet too far from the falconer
   to hear instructions of its failure, that
Turns within its gyre a hundred downward
   turns, proud and tired but finally bored, so we
   descended to that place all fire has claimed,   120
The monster Geryon gliding to the floor,
   settling at last and close to the rocky
   source of Hell's eighth precipice, and from here,
Relieved of the live weight on his back,
Disappearing like an arrow into the dark.   125

CANTO XVIII / *Stanley Plumly*

In Hell there is a great and giving ground
　　called Malebolge, of stone the color of
　　the pig iron in the high stone wall that guards
It, in the center of which an abyss
　　opens up, all breadth and endless evil depth,　　　5
　　whose structure I will offer up in sequence.
Therefore the margin in between the great pit
　　and the high hard wall is one wide circle
　　with ten descending valleys terraced—cut—
Into the bottom, creating in a　　　10
　　kind of castle theme deep successive moats
　　meant to be defenses but with bridges
Over emptiness from threshold to pitch
　　toward some final bank, these bridging arches
　　wavelike from the wall ending in the pit,　　　15
Their common center. So we found ourselves
　　dropped here, once Geryon set us down, my guide
　　to the left of where I walked behind, as
On the right below in the first of the
　　empty moats, new misery, new torments,　　　20
　　new naked souls, in the pattern of a
Lockstep—some on our side of the middle
　　walking toward us, others on the other
　　side in our same direction but quickly,
The way the Romans, the year of Jubilee,　　　25
　　to keep the crowds in motion, divided
　　their passage on the bridge in half: all eyes:
Those headed to St. Peter's, toward the Castle,
　　those headed in the opposite, the Mount.
　　And left and right, along the awful　　　30

Ditch, I saw horned demons practicing their
   whips, lashing the nameless backs of souls—
   and how the loafers at the straggler's
End paid for their slowness at the first whip
   crack, quick-step, quick-step, until they all were   35
   ahead of the second and the third tip.
Then one whom I recognized seemed to know
   me. I said, as if in speaking past him,
   "I think I once knew this one well," and so
I stopped to study him, and my master,   40
   in his patience, also stopped and kindly
   let me step back a little to get closer.
But this lost soul, hoping to hide himself
   by looking down, was only obvious—
   "You who cast your eyes into the ground, whose   45
Face I know, are Venedico Caccianimico;
   why are you here among this slow boil of pain?"
   He answered me: "If I could I would say no,
But your voice in which I hear the vital
   world again, arrests me. I was the one   50
   who sold Ghisolabella to the Marquis' will,
However else you hear the whoring details
   of the story. I'm not the only Bolognese
   weeping in this place; we so fill it full
That not so many tongues have learned to say   55
   sipa between the Savena and Reno,
   as if you didn't know from memory
The degree of our famous avarice."
   And even while he spoke the lash was laid—
   "Pimp, move on, you'll find no women to seduce   60
Along this path." Then I turned from him and
   again joined my master, where, in a few
   more steps, we came to a stark rock bridging
Promontory that we climbed easily
   and followed to its right, by way of leaving   65
   these rock-bound, sad, and eternal circlings.

And when we reached the passage in the stone
  cut for the sinners under lash, my guide
  said, "Stay awhile to take the sight of those
Now coming into view, whose faces were   70
  obscure because they've been behind us,
  these dead souls, these ghosts of flesh, these users."
So from this bridge we looked down the column
  driven forward from the other side,
  the stinging of the whip no less laid on.   75
My master volunteered: "See that great one
  coming, who handles pain without the pain
  of tears, how he looks the king, this Jason,
Who by courage and device relieved the men
  of Colchis of the Fleece; who later, when   80
  he happened past the strange isle of Lemnos,
Where the loveless women in their anger
  put all their men to death, spread honey
  on his words to gull the famed beguiler
Hypsipyle, she who would save her father.   85
  Jason left her there, pregnant, forsaken.
  His guilt condemns him now, and even more
Through vengence of Medea. The slavery
  with him are deceivers too. It's enough
  to see them swallowed within this valley."   90
By now we were already where the path
  narrows and crosses the second bank that
  serves as basis for yet another bridge,
And here we heard the whining in the next
  ditch, the snorting of snouts, the flat dead palms   95
  beating against the purging of dead flesh.
Like steam or vapor from a stinking pit,
  their exhalations rose in humid air
  so thick they stuck and crusted over, sick
To the eye and nose: that bottom sinking   100
  deep beyond our sight, until we got to
  the bridgelike crown of the arch overhang

That permitted us to see these human
   forms mired in their excrement, as if in
   a tidal flow from human privies.   105
My eyes, compelled to search among this scene,
   saw one bare head so covered up in shit
   you couldn't tell if it was lay or clergy. . .
The head spoke out: "Why do you stare at me
   more than at these others just as foul?"   110
   "Because," I said, "if I remember well,
I knew you once from when your hair was dry—
   you are Alessio Interminei of Lucca—
   and so of course you suddenly stood out."
And as if it were almost not quite his,   115
   he beat his head. "Down here my flatteries
   turn into their value as human waste."
And at that moment my good master said,
   "Lean forward a little beyond these here
   to see the one over there who scratches   120
Herself with her shit-packed nails, and fidgets
   constantly, first squatting down, then standing
   up—it's Thaïs the whore, who once answered
Her lover's question about the value
   of the pleasure he bestowed by saying,   125
   bitterly, it was joy beyond value.
Now let us turn away from these lost souls
And away from the emptiness they fill."

CANTO XIX / *C. K. Williams*

O, Simon Magus, you
  and all of your
  rapacious followers,
  those wretched robbers, who,
  for gold and silver,   5
  whore
Away the things of God
  that should be wedded
  unto righteousness;
  all of you, bedded
  in the third pit: 10
  listen to the trumpet!
We, in the meantime,
  arrived at the next tomb,
  on the cornice
  of rock which looms   15
  out over the center
  of the crevasse.
O, highest wisdom,
  in heaven, earth, and
  even in this evil place,   20
  how justly you impart
  your power, how manifest
  yourself with so much art!
I saw that in the livid
  stone were holes,   25
  across the bottom
  and up along the sides,
  all round, all
  the same size.

They seemed to be   30
    as wide, and have
    a similar capacity
    as the baptismal
    baths in my lovely
    San Giovanni . . .   35
One of which not many
    years ago I broke,
    to save somebody drowning:
    any gossip
    otherwise let this   40
    declaration stop.
From each hole's mouth,
    a sinner stuck,
    but only half;
    just the feet   45
    and legs showed,
    and only to the calf.
The soles of their feet
    were on fire,
    and their joints convulsed   50
    with so much power,
    they'd have snapped rope,
    or baling wire.
As flame will flow
    on oil-soaked things,   55
    lightly on the surface, so
    it slithered here,
    back and forth,
    from heel to toe.
"Master," I said,   60
    "who is that
    who twitches and trembles
    more than the rest,
    and who a brighter
    red flame sucks at?"   65

And he replied:
  "If you'll let me lead you
  along that precipitous shelf,
  you can hear about
  his crimes   70
  from him himself."
Then I: "What pleases you
  also pleases me;
  I accept your will;
  you know, too,   75
  what I don't have to say:
  I want what you do."
So we descended
  once more,
  down the fourth embankment   80
  and then left
  across the narrow
  perforated floor.
My good teacher
  kept me next to him,   85
  not letting me go
  until we'd reached
  the hole of him whose
  legs lamented so.
"Who are you?" I began.   90
  "Unhappy soul,
  planted like a pole
  with your upper
  part down: answer
  if you can."   95
I stood like a friar,
  a vile assassin,
  fixed head-first in
  the ground, will plead
  to confess to again,   100
  to delay being buried.

"Are you standing there
  already, Boniface?"
  he cried.
  "Is it you,   105
  years ahead of time?
  Have the prophesies lied?
Are you so quickly sated
  by that wealth you took
  from the lovely lady, so   110
  shamelessly, with such deceit,
  then so outrageously
  proceeded to mistreat?"
I stood like someone
  someone else is mocking,   115
  who can't grasp the way
  the other speaks,
  or why, and can't think
  of what to say.
Virgil told me then,   120
  "Say: I'm not him,
  I'm not the one you think;
  tell him he's misguided:
  tell him right away,"
  and so I did.   125
At which the spirit
  spasmed both his feet
  again, and then
  sighed tearfully,
  "What do you want   130
  of me?
If it's so important
  that you'd cross the bank
  in the hope
  of knowing who I am,   135
  know it then: I wore
  the mantle of the pope.

A true son of the bear,
   eager to advance my cubs,
   I stuffed money in my pocket   140
   while I lived up there,
   and stuffed myself
   into another pocket here.
Underneath my head
   all those preceding me   145
   who dared condone
   the sin of simony
   are crushed in fissures
   in the stone.
And I'll be tamped   150
   down further, too,
   when he arrives
   whom I mistook you for
   when I abruptly
   questioned you.   155
I've broiled my feet
   upside down, though,
   longer than the time
   that will expire
   with him planted so,   160
   his feet afire,
Because after him a lawless
   shepherd will come
   out of the west, whose deeds
   are of such ugliness   165
   that he'll be qualified
   to cover both of us.
He'll be another Jason,
   who, we're told in Maccabees,
   found a pliant king   170
   and realized his chance . . .
   so will this one,
   with the king of France."

Here I thought I might
   be being rash,   175
   going past a limit,
   because I answered him like this:
   "How much wealth
   would be your estimate
Our Lord demanded   180
   that Saint Peter give
   to have the keys
   placed in his authority?
   All that he found necessary
   was a 'Follow me.'   185
And neither did Peter
   or the others ask Matthias
   what the cost
   would be in gold or silver
   for the office the betraying   190
   soul had lost.
Stay where you are, less
   well punished than you
   should be, keep close watch
   on the fraudulent gains   195
   that made you so audacious
   against Charles.
And if it weren't
   forbidden me
   by the reverence I still feel   200
   for those great keys
   which in the better life
   were your property,
My words would
   be harsher still: 205
   all of you, your avarice
   afflicts the world,
   trampling the good,
   exalting the unscrupulous.

It was shepherds like you   210
   the Evangelist was thinking
   of when he saw her
   who sits upon the waters
   fornicating
   with the kings,   215
She who was born
   with seven heads,
   and drew support
   from her ten horns,
   as long as it was virtue   220
   that inspired her consort.
You've made a god
   of gold and silver;
   are you outdone
   by those who worship   225
   idols? You have a hundred,
   they at least just one.
Ah, Constantine, all
   the evil brought to birth,
   not by your conversion,   230
   but when you bestowed on
   that first wealthy father
   half the earth."
As I incanted
   these notes to him,   235
   whether it was conscience
   gnawing him, or angry heat,
   he was kicking hard
   with both his feet.
And I think the sound   240
   of the truths I was telling
   pleased my guide;
   his expression
   as he listened
   seemed quite satisfied.   245

He lifted me, and then,
   when I was tight
   against his breast,
   he turned to the path
   we'd descended,   250
   and we started up again.
Never wearying,
   he didn't stop
   until he'd carried me
   to the arch of the fourth   255
   and fifth walls,
   then to its top.
Here he gently
   set his burden down;
   gently, since the scree   260
   was steep and rough,
   hard going
   even for a chamois,
And here another valley
Was revealed to me.   265

CANTO XX / *Robert Pinsky*

The new pains of Hell that I saw next demand
   new lines for this Canto XX of the first Canzon,
   which is of those submerged in the underground.
Readying myself at the cliff's brink, I looked down
   into the canyon my master had revealed   5
   and saw that it was watered by tears of pain.
All through the circular valley I beheld
   a host of people parading, weeping but mute.
   They walked at a solemn pace that would be called
Liturgical here above. But as my sight   10
   moved down their bodies, I sensed a strange distortion
   that made the angle of chin and chest not right—
The head was twisted backwards: some cruel torsion
   forced face toward kidneys, so the people strode
   backwards, all being deprived of forward vision.   15
Possibly some time a palsy has wrung the head
   of a man straight back like these, or a terrible stroke—
   but I've never seen one do so, and doubt it could.
Reader, God grant you benefit of this book,
   try to imagine, yourself, whether I kept   20
   tears of my own from falling for the sake
Of our human image so grotesquely reshaped,
   contorted so the eyes' tears fell to wet
   the buttocks at the cleft. Truly I wept,
Leaning on an outcrop of that rocky site,   25
   and my master spoke to me: "Do you suppose
   you are above with the other fools even yet?
Here, pity lives when it is dead to these.
   Who could be more impious than one who'd dare
   to sorrow at the judgment God decrees?   30

Raise your head—raise it and see one walking near
  for whom the earth split open before the eyes
  of all the Thebans. 'Why are you leaving the war,
Amphiaraus,' the others shouted, 'what place
  are you away to?' as he plunged down the crevice   35
  to Minos, who seizes all. Now Amphiaraus
Must make his shoulders his breast; because his purpose
  was seeing too far ahead, he looks behind
  and stumbles backwards. And here is Tiresias,
The seer who changed from male to female, unmanned   40
  through all his body until the day he struck
  a second time with his staff at serpents entwined
And resumed his manly plumage. He with his back
  shoved nose to the other's front is called Aruns:
  Living on the slopes the Carrarese work   45
From villages below, he had clear vistas—
  from his cave among white marble scanning the stars
  or gazing at waves below him in the distance.
And she, whose loose hair hides her breasts but bares
  on that same side the other places hair grows,   50
  was Manto, who searching many regions made hers
The land where I was born—and now for a space
  I mean to tell you about it: after Tiresias,
  her father, died and Thebes was enslaved, she chose
To roam the world. Where a wall of mountains rises   55
  to form fair Italy's border above Tirolo
  lies Lake Benaco, fed by a thousand sources:
Garda and Val Camonica and Pennino
  are watered by streams that settle into that lake.
  Amid them, a spot the pastor of Trentino   60
May bless—or Brescia or Verona, should they seek
  where their three bishoprics meet. At the shore's low place,
  Peschiera's splendid fortress towers make
Their challenge to the Brescians and Bergamese.
  There, all the cascades Benaco cannot contain   65
  within its bosom join in one river that flows

Through rich green pasture. As soon as it starts to run,
  the water, Benaco no more, is Mincio instead,
  and joining the Po at Govèrnolo, it soon
Spreads to a marsh—in summer, sometimes fetid.   70
  There Manto the savage virgin saw in mid-fen
  a stretch of dry land, untilled, uninhabited,
And there the she-mage settled, where she could shun
  all humans to ply her arts in a place she shared
  only with her servants. And when her life was gone   75
And her soul descended, there its shell was interred.
  Afterwards, families scattered about that country
  gathered where marsh on all sides made a ward
Against attackers. And when they built their city
  on her bones they named it Mantua, after the pagan   80
  sorceress who chose it. Before fool Casalodi
Was deceived by Pinamonte, its population
  was larger. Now I have told the unclouded truth
  of my city's birth—believe no other version."
I: "Master, to me your words are certain. My faith   85
  in what you tell me is perfect, contradiction
  would be burnt-out coals to me, a husk of myth—
But speak again of these souls in sad procession:
  are any passing below us worthy of note?
  For my mind keeps turning back in that direction."   90
Then he: "That one, whose beard has spread in a mat
  across his olive shoulders, was augur when Greece
  was short of males. He divined the time to cut
The first ship's cable at Aulis, along with Calchas.
  His name, as my tragedy sings—of course you know   95
  the passage, who know it entirely—is Eurypylus.
That other with skinny flanks is Michael Scotto,
  master magician and celebrated fraud.
  There's Guido Bonatti, and there's Asdente, who now
Wishes he'd stuck to leather and cobbler's thread,   100
  instead of his astrological predictions.
  And this wretched crowd of women all chose to trade

Loom, spindle and thimble for the telling of fortunes,
    potions, wax images, incantation and charm.
    But come: already, Cain-in-the-moon positions   105
Both hemispheres with his pale blue thorns, his term
    closes in the waves below Seville—the round moon
    that, deep in the wood last night, brought you no harm."
Even while he spoke the words, we were moving on.

CANTO XXI / *Susan Mitchell*

And so from bridge to bridge we went, talking,
 but not of things I mean to sing to all
 the world; and talking brought us to the top
Where we stopped and took in the next crevasse
 of Malebolge: Oh, those ghostly cries!   5
 It was preternaturally dark—
You know what it's like in the shipyards of Venice,
 how all winter workers boil the pitch
 to caulk and patch up their leaky ships
When storms keep them off the roughened seas: 10
 one hammers out a new boat, one plugs
 the cracked seams of an old sea-worn vessel,
One strikes the stern, another bangs on the prow,
 some make oars, others are braiding rope,
 another repairs the main, someone the lug sail;   15
Well, not with fire, but with immortal heat
 a thick pitch is boiling down there and sticks
 like glue to both banks of the river.
I saw it. But I could not see in it
 anything but huge bubbles the boiling raised.   20
 The mess kept swelling up, then sinking back.
As if hypnotized, I kept staring down
 until my leader cried out, "Watch it! Watch it!"
 and pulled me back to safety just in time:
That's when I turned, dying to have a look   25
 at the very thing I should have run from;
 yet at that moment I was seized with fear,
I was running and looking at the same time.
 And there behind us running up along
 the spiny ridge was a black devil.   30

[96]

How wild he looked, how menacing to me
   his every movement, with leathery wings
   spread wide open, and almost flying on his feet.
His shoulder was weighed down by a sinner he'd slung
   across it, and he held the wretch by both his ankles,   35
   the way a butcher carries a side of beef.
Then from our bridge he called, "Evil Claws,
   I've got a new one for you from Santa Zita.
   Stick him below, I'm going back for more!
That city is well stocked with the likes of him.   40
   Except for Bonturo, everyone's on the take
   and for a bribe will change a 'no' to 'yes.'"
He flung the wretch down, then ran back along
   the cliff: never was a dog set loose
   in such a hurry to catch a thief.   45
The sinner he had hurled, heaved up, doubled
   over with pain. But the devils by the bridge
   taunted, "You won't find Old Holy Face here!
Don't think you're swimming in that pure stream,
   the Serchio, and if you don't want to feel   50
   our hooks, stay down in the steaming pitch."
At once they gripped him with a hundred hooks:
   "Here the dance is done under cover,
   so snatch some on the sly, if you can."
Just like the servant boys of cooks, they hooked   55
   this meat and shoved him deep into the boiling
   pot: they made certain he wouldn't float.
My good master said, "Crouch down behind
   that jagged rock so it won't seem you're here.
   You'll need that shield to hide from them.   60
And no matter how they menace me,
   don't be afraid, I've got this under control.
   This isn't the first scuffle I've had."
Once he told me what to do, he left
   and as he walked alone to the sixth bank,   65
   he made an effort to appear composed.

But the devils, with the frenzy and commotion
   dogs make when they go after some luckless wretch
   who has to beg right there where he stands,
Those devils rushed out from under the bridge   70
   and turned all their forks against my guide.
   "Not one of you dare touch me," he cried.
"Before you savage me with those forks
   one of you had better listen well—
   then decide whether you want to stick me."   75
"You go, Knife Tail," all of them were screaming
   so that one moved on up while the rest stayed back
   muttering, "A lot of good it will do him."
But my guide: "Do you really think, Knife Tail,
   when you've seen me come here safe and sound,   80
   unharmed by any of your wild schemes,
I don't have divine help on my side?
   Let us move on, that's the will of Heaven.
   It's fated I show another this savage place."
At that the devil lost his proud look.   85
   He let his fork fall to the ground and said:
   "Well, in that case, we'll have to let him go."
Then my guide called me where I sat huddled
   and crouching among the jagged rocks of the bridge:
   "You can feel safe now and come back to me."   90
At this I stirred and came to him fast as I could.
   But the devils all moved forward too,
   so that I doubted they would keep their word.
If you saw the infantry marching out
   under safe conduct from Caprona,   95
   saw men trembling as they passed their enemies,
You'll know how I huddled up against my guide.
   Not for a moment did I look away
   from the menacing looks those devils gave us;
Though they lowered their hooks, still one jeered: 100
   "Should I stick him up his behind?" And all
   the others, "Yes, yes! Give it to him!"

But the devil who had been talking
   with my guide spun around and cried,
   "Down, Slob, get down!"   105
Then to us: "There's no way to go much further
   along the ridge because the sixth arch
   of the bridge is smashed to pieces at the bottom.
So if you still want to go on ahead,
   move up and walk along this rocky ledge: 110
   there's a cliff nearby where you'll find a path.
At noon yesterday, by my reckoning, exactly
   twelve hundred and sixty-six years had come and gone
   since this road was shattered and left in ruins.
I'm sending some of my men on ahead   115
   to see if some sinner dare stick up his head
   for air. Go with them—they won't harm you.
Hey you, Buffoon, and you, Ancient Foot,
   you too, Dog Face," he called to the devils,
   "and you, Curly Beard, lead the squad.   120
Let Windy go and also Dragon Smile,
   then Hog-With-Tusks and also Dog Scratcher.
   Then the Scamp, and you too, Crazy Mad.
Search through the steaming pitch and keep these two
   safe from harm, at least to the next ridge   125
   that rises over our caves and hideouts."
I said, "Master, must they? Can't we go on
   without their company? Especially
   since you know the way, let's skip the escort.
If you were as shrewd as you usually are,   130
   you'd see how those devils gnash their teeth.
   With darkened brows they threaten us with harm."
Then my guide said: "Don't be afraid.
   Let them chomp and grind as much as they want
   to cook up a scare in their stew of sinners." 135
The devils turned to take the left-hand bank.
   But first each stuck out his tongue between his teeth,
   which I took for a signal to their leader.
As reply he made a bugle of his ass.

CANTO XXII / *Susan Mitchell*

Think of the cavalry breaking camp to start
  the assault, think of horsemen rounded up,
  horses prancing out, then a hasty retreat.
I've seen scouts ranging your land, Aretines,
  seen foraging parties, the shock of battle, rush   5
  of wind as jousters clashed, lances shivering.
With a shout of trumpets and bells wildly ringing,
  with a thrill of drums and signals smoked from castles,
  with household rags, outlandish contraptions,
I've seen cavaliers and troops set out   10
  and ships that navigate by stars and seaside towers—
  but no one ever set off with such strange homemade music.
Well, we had ten devils as our escort.
  And what a company that was! But in church
  you sing with the saints, in the tavern with guzzlers.   15
I kept staring at the churning pitch
  so I wouldn't miss a single sound
  or gesture of the people burning there.
You know how dolphins will leap and flash
  their arched backs when a storm is brewing, so sailors   20
  know it's time to save their ships from fierce waves—
That's how the back of a sinner will hunch up
  as he tries to get relief from his pain.
  Then quick as lightning he'll sink down again.
And you know how at a ditch's scummy edge   25
  frogs will pout and puff with just their snouts
  on view (their plump bellies are well submerged)—
Here the sinners peer up at you like that.
  But whenever Curly Beard approached,
  they sank back into the seething pitch.   30

I saw, and even remembering makes me shudder,
  a wretch who stayed above too long, like a frog
  that remains when it ought to dive with the others.
Dog Scratcher caught sight of him, and grabbed
  the sinner by his tar-smeared hair, dragged   35
  him out, matted and dripping like an otter.
By this time I knew all the devils' names—
  I had listened carefully as their chief
  called each one forward. Now I heard:
"Get him, Crazy Mad! Sink your claws   40
  into his back, rip him up and down!"
  All the fiends were screaming this together.
I said, "Master, see if you can find out
  the name of the sinner who has fallen prey
  to that savage pack of guard dogs." My guide   45
At once approached the unlucky offender and asked
  him where he was from. "I was born," he said,
  "in the Kingdom of Navarre, and my mother
Had me by a good-for-nothing scoundrel
  who destroyed himself and all he owned.   50
  Next, she placed me in the service of a lord,
And later, in the household of a king, the good Thibaut;
  it was there I started taking bribes.
  Now I'm hot to pay for what was paid me."
Then Hog-With-Tusks, who had real boar's tusks   55
  pushing out of his jaws, let the sinner
  feel how these could slash and mangle.
Well, the cats had their mouse to play with.
  Curly Beard got to him first and cried,
  "Stay where you are. He's mine now."   60
Then turning to my master, the devil said:
  "If you want to learn more from him, ask now,
  Before the others disjoint him."
My guide asked him then, "Those other sinners
  still deep in the pitch—are any from Italy?"   65
  "I have just left one," he said, "from a place

Not far from there, and how I wish I were still
    boiling with him—then at least I wouldn't
    have to fear these devils' hooks and claws."
"This is the last straw," said Windy. "We've put up   70
    with too much from him already," and with his hook
    he ripped from the other's arm a sinewy strip of muscle.
Now Dragon Smile tried to grab hold of the sinner's
    legs from below, but the chief put a stop to this
    with a single dark and scowling look.   75
That calmed them down, and losing no time, my guide
    turned to the one still staring at his wound,
    saying, "Who was it you left down there
To come ashore, that one you mentioned leaving
    when you were foolish enough to come up for air?"   80
    "Fra Gomita of Gallura," came the reply,
"Now he was a pot boiling over with dirty schemes.
    He held his master's enemies in the palm of his hand,
    but managed it so well, even they sang his praises.
He took their bribes, and as he tells it, easily   85
    had their cases settled out of court.
    All in all, he was the king of swindlers.
You'll find with him Don Michele Zanche
    of Logodoro: those two never get tired
    of talking about the times they had in Sardinia.   90
But look! Do you see that fiend over there, gnashing
    his teeth. I'd say more if I weren't afraid
    he's getting ready to tear me apart."
The chief devil saw that too: "Get away,
    you bird-brain," he yelled at Scamp, the fiend   95
    so eager to fight his eyes started from his head.
"If," began the sinner terrified, "if
    you wish to speak with Tuscans or Lombards
    I can get a few to come up here.
But the Evil Claws must stand back a bit   100
    so that my friends won't have to fear their vengeance.
    Without moving an inch, I can make

A good seven appear just by giving
    a special whistle—that's our signal here
    to say the coast is clear to come ashore." 105
At these words, Dog Face shook his head and snarled,
    "Just listen to him! Does he really think
    he can skip out on us with a trick like that?"
The sinner, who had more than one trick up his sleeve,
    replied, "I'd really be the worst of scoundrels 110
    if I were to think of tricking my own friends."
At this Buffoon couldn't keep back his rage:
    "If you dive down there and give us the slip
    I won't just run after you, I'll fly."
But still he agreed to "go down the bank 115
    to where the overhang will hide us.
    Then we'll see if you're a match for fiends."
Now listen, Reader, here's a brand-new game.
    The devils all agreed to look away.
    And even the wary Dog Face led the pack. 120
But the Navarrese saw his chance—and jumped,
    in the blink of an eye was free from the hellish chief,
    who hadn't held him tight enough. At this
The devils burned with shame, especially Buffoon
    who'd brought disgrace on all the rest. He leaped 125
    after the sinner, screaming, "Got you!" Little
Good it did him. Fear needs no wings to fly.
    By then the sinner had submerged, and the devil,
    miffed, could only flap his wings. Picture
A duck as a hawk comes swooping down. See 130
    how the duck dives under, leaving the hawk to fly off
    all ruffled and out of sorts: that's just how these two looked.
The trick made Ancient Foot go wild, and he
    gave chase, eager to have the sinner
    escape, so he'd have a reason to fight Buffoon. 135
For now that the Navarrese had taken cover,
    he had only Buffoon to sink his claws into
    and grapple with above the seething ditch.

But Buffoon was a fierce, well-made hawk, his talons
   could grip and tear and rip, and now the two,   140
   still grappling, fell, all tangled up, into
The pitch below. The heat unsnarled them there.
   Still, they had no way to get out:
   their wings were stuck fast in the burning glue.
All the devils grieved, but Curly Beard   145
   was quick to dispatch fiends with a batch of hooks
   to the other bank, where soon enough
They took their posts; then four to each side,
   they held out their hooks and forked up that pair
   of birds—by now well cooked inside their skins.   150
We left the others to clean up the mess.

CANTO XXIII / *Carolyn Forché*

We went on alone in silence without them
    as Brothers of our order, one ahead
    and one behind, and my thoughts were on
Aesop's fable of the frog and mouse. *Now*
    and *at present* aren't more alike than these two   5
    stories, if you consider how they begin and end
And as one thought gives rise to another, another
    rose, this one even more chilling. "Because of us
    they've been humiliated, adding insult to injury.
They're evil to begin with,   10
    and in their rage and pain, they'll come
    after us like dogs after rabbits."
Just then I felt my hair bristle and, glancing
    behind, I said, "Master, I'm afraid of the Malebranche,
    can't you hide us? I imagine them so well I hear them coming."   15
He answered, "If I were a mirror I wouldn't
    reflect your fears as quickly as I have imagined
    them. We are alike. Just now your thoughts
Entered among mine and were my own, and in them
    I hear an answer: If that right bank isn't too steep   20
    we'll climb into the next ravine and escape this chase."
He hadn't finished when I saw them coming,
    wings open, closing the distance, intent on us.
    My guide lifted me, as a mother in a burning house
Lifts her child, naked, unthinking, more concerned   25
    for the child than for herself, and leapt down the bank
    sliding on the bare rock blocking the next passage.
Water never rushed through a sluice to slap the paddles
    of a waterwheel so fast as he fled with me
    more his son than a friend now, down the bank.   30

We had yet to reach bottom when ten demons
   appeared on the ridge above us. But we, now safe
   in the ravine, felt great relief
The Will that gave them charge over the fifth ditch
   forbids them to leave it, and so they remained   35
   on the fifth ridge, powerless.
Below, we found painted people moving slowly,
   dragging themselves from exhaustion, weeping,
   wearing cloaks like the monks' robes of Cluny.
These hooded robes were brilliantly gilded   40
   but lined in lead so heavy that those Frederick
   the King made men wear seemed straw.
A tiring cape for eternity!
   We turned, always to the left along with them,
   fixed upon their grief.   45
But they walked so slowly under their lead robes
   that the more we walked, the more they fell behind
   and with every step, we caught up with others.
So I asked my guide to find a famous one among them
   if he could, someone known for what he did or   50
   who he was, with whom I might have a word.
And one who heard my Tuscan language cried,
   "Wait! Slow down. You two, running so fast
   through this filthy air.
Maybe I can tell you what you wish to know."   55
   My guide turned to me: "Wait, then walk
   beside him at his pace."
I stopped, and saw two who seemed to want to talk,
   but they were slowed by the narrow path
   and the weight of their robes.   60
When they reached me, they shot sideways looks
   and seemed silenced by the weight until they leaned
   toward one another never taking their eyes from me.
"This one's alive. Look at his throat.
   And if not, if he is dead, then why no robe?   65
   By what privilege are these two exempt?"

Then they said to me, "Tuscan! You've come
  to this gathering of hypocrites—don't be afraid to tell
  us who you are."
And I answered, "I was born in Arno and grew up   70
  in the great town on the Arno river, and this body
  is the body I've always had.
But you. Who are you, standing there
  in tears? And what is that robe
  you wear as a shining punishment?"   75
And one of them said, "These mandarin
  cloaks are made of lead so heavy that we, the scales
  beneath them, groan under their weight.
We were two happy brothers in the city
  of Bologna. Catalano was my name   80
  and his, Loderingo. We were charged
With keeping the peace in your city, two men
  where one would have done, and what peace
  we kept is obvious around Gardingo."
"Brothers," I began, "what atrocities,"   85
  but was silenced by the sight of a crucified man
  pinned by three stakes to the ground.
When he saw me, he writhed in agony
  and sighed deeply into his beard,
  and seeing that, Brother Catalano said,   90
"That one you see impaled there
  counseled the Pharisees that it was prudent
  to let one man rather than a whole nation suffer.
Naked, stretched across the path
  as you see, he is condemned to feel the weight   95
  of everyone who passes over him, and all they bear.
In the same ravine, his father-in-law
  and the others are stretched the same, those
  who planted the seed of blood for the Jews."
Then I saw Virgil, standing in awe above the one   100
  who lay stretched on the path
  of eternal exile.

[107]

And he told the brothers this:
   "If you don't mind, please, if you may,
   tell us if there is a way out of here.   105
Any fissure in the rock where we might slip
   without our having to ask the black angels
   to come to our rescue?"
"Nearer than you could hope," he answered,
   "You'll find a ridge of rock that juts   110
   from the great wall and forms a path
Through all these evil valleys, but here the path
   is broken, and there, where the ruins drop along
   the bank and pile, you can climb out."
My guide stood with his head bent down   115
   and then said, "He lied to us back there,
   that guard charged with hooking sinners."
And to this the Brother said, "In Bologna,
   they said the devil, among other things,
   was a liar and the father of lies."   120
My guide hurried away, disturbed, angry,
   and seeing this I left those burdened souls,
   following my Master in his steps.

CANTO XXIV / *Carolyn Forché*

In early spring, when the sun enters
   Aquarius, rinsing its bright hair,
   and the nights shorten toward the south;
When, on the ground, frost copies his sister
   the snow, but with a pen so dull that only   5
   brief traces of his sketch remain;
The farmer with no food in his cellar
   wakes and looks out over the white fields,
   strikes himself in despair, then
Returns to his bed but can't be still   10
   and can't do much of anything, so paces
   in grief, poor man, and once more looks outside
This time in hope, when he sees how much
   the earth has changed in hours, then he takes
   his stick to the field to drive the lambs. So there,   15
When I saw the despair in my guide's face
   my spirits filled with dread, until as quickly
   as fear had come, its wound was bandaged:
When we reached the ruined bridge, my guide
   looked at me the same sweet way he did   20
   in the beginning, and after
Some thought, and after poking in the ruins,
   he took me in his arms like one who works
   and knows which steps to take, and lifted me
Over one great rock while edging toward another,   25
   saying, "Try this next, but test it first
   to see if it will bear your weight."
That was no place for a leaden cloak, for even we—
   he weightless and I helped up—hardly made it
   from one rock to another.   30

Had it not been that this wall sloped less
   I don't know what would have happened
   to him, but I surely would have fallen.
But because Malebolge runs into the mouth
   of the farthest well, each valley has walls   35
   both high and low, and we finally came
To the last rock, where I lost my breath
   and sat, weak on the wall
   until my guide arrived.
"What laziness," he cried, "aren't you ashamed?   40
   Sitting on your down bed wrapped in blankets
   is no way to get through life.
Anyone who lives that way leaves
   no more of himself on earth than
   smoke on air or foam on water.   45
Get up, get hold of yourself.
   Your soul has put up with you this long,
   and there's a higher ladder to climb
What we've done is not enough. If you
   understand what I'm saying, show me you're   50
   willing to devote the necessary time."
I stood, breathing more deeply than I thought
   I could, and I answered "Go as you wish,
   I'm strong and determined."
We took a thin, rugged route up the ridge,   55
   a steeper, more difficult way than we'd taken before
   and I talked as we went so as not to seem tired,
When a voice rose out of the pit barely able to speak,
   and I don't know what it said, but I was
   already at the edge, and the voice was angry.   60
I was bending to look down, but my eyes
   couldn't make out anything in that dark;
   so I said, "Master, let's go on
To the next wall and go down.
   From here I can't see anything,   65
   and I can't make out a sound."

"My only answer," he said, "is action.
 When a reasonable request is made,
 the only just reply is a silent act."
So we moved down the bridge to the pier   70
 of the eighth bank, and then the ditch
 was clear to me: a snake pit
With great coils of serpents so strange
 that the memory of them roiling
 chills my blood.   75
Let Libya brag no longer, for her deserts
 breed chelidrids, jaculi and phareans,
 cenchriads, and two-headed ampisbands,
But she never bred this much variety,
 not with all of Ethiopia nor all the lands   80
 bordering the Red Sea.
People were running naked among the snakes
 without hope of escape, nor so much as
 a heliotrope or hiding place.
Their hands were tied behind their backs with serpents   85
 that thrust their heads and tails into their loins
 and were tied into a writhing knot in front.
One of the damned came hurrying around a rock
 and a serpent rose and sank its fangs
 into him where the neck meets the shoulder.   90
No one has ever written the letters *o* or *i*
 as quickly as that soul burst into flames
 and fell to ash
And when he was utterly destroyed
 on the ground, the dust gathered itself   95
 into his former shape
Just as philosophers thought:
 the Phoenix dies and is reborn
 when it reaches its five hundredth year.
It lives on tears of balsam and incense,   100
 and never eats herbs or grain,
 its burial clothes are scented with nard and myrrh.

And as one who falls without knowing why,
    by force of a demon dragging him down,
    or some other impediment blocking him,   105
When he rises, and looks about
    confused by the agony he's suffered
    and sighs, that is how this one rose.
O power of God! How terrible it is,
    showering such fearful   110
    blows in revenge.
Then my guide asked him who he was
    and he answered, "A short while ago
    I rained down from Tuscany into this gulley.
A beast's life rather than a human one pleased me,   115
    ass that I was. I am Vanni Fucci, the beast.
    Wild Pistoia was my den."
And I said to my guide, "Tell him not to go,
    and ask what sin he committed.
    I knew him as a man of blood and rage."   120
And the sinner who heard me didn't flinch,
    but gazed at me directly, red with shame,
    and said, "It makes me sadder that you caught me
Here in this misery than I was when I died.
    I can't refuse to answer you. I am here   125
    because I stole riches from the sacristy,
And let others take the blame. But I'll tell you
    something, and if you should ever
    get out of here, you'll see that what
I tell you will come true: 130
    first Pistoia will expel members of the Black Party;
    then new rulers in Florence will change her laws
From Valdimagra, the fiery smoke of war
    will rise into the air, then in the storm
    of battle on Piceno's fields   135
War will tear the clouds apart
    and every White will be wounded.
    There you have it, may you die of grief.

CANTO XXV / *Richard Wilbur*

The thief, when he had done with prophecy,
   made figs of both his lifted hands, and cried,
   "Take these, O God, for they are aimed at Thee!"
Then was my heart upon the serpents' side,
   for round his neck one coiled like a garrotte   5
   as if to say, "Enough of ranting pride,"
And another pinned his arms, and tied a knot
   of head and tail in front of him again,
   so tightly that they could not stir one jot.
Alas, Pistoia, why dost thou not ordain   10
   that thou be burnt to ashes, since thou hast
   out-sinned the base begetters of thy strain?
In the dark rounds of Hell through which I passed,
   I saw no spirit so blaspheme his Lord,
   not him who from the Theban wall was cast.   15
He fled then, speaking not another word,
   and into sight a raging centaur came:
   "Where has that half-cooked sinner gone?" he roared.
So many snakes Maremma cannot claim
   as covered all his back in dense array,   20
   to where his form took on a human frame.
Behind his nape, upon his shoulders, lay
   a seething dragon with its wings outspread,
   which sets afire whatever comes its way.
"Him you behold is Cacus," my master said,   25
   "who underneath the rock of the Aventine
   so often made a lake of bloody red.
He is not with his brothers, since condign
   justice has set him here, who to his den
   so craftily made off with Geryon's kine: 30

[*113*]

For that, his crooked ways were ended then
   by the club of Hercules, which dealt him nigh
   a hundred blows, of which he felt not ten."
While thus he spoke, the centaur hastened by,
   and from below three spirits came in view,   35
   whose coming neither my great guide nor I
Perceived until they shouted, "Who are you?"
   At that, we two broke off our talk together
   and turned our whole attention to that crew.
Who they might be I did not promptly gather;   40
   but, as may chance in meetings of the kind,
   one had occasion then to name another,
Saying, "Where's Cianfa? Why did he fall behind?"
   I put my finger to my lips, to show
   my guide that he should wait and pay them mind.   45
'Twill be no wonder, Reader, if you are slow
   to trust the thing that I shall now impart,
   for I, who saw it, scarce believe it so.
I watched a vile, six-footed serpent dart
   toward one of them, and then, with never a pause,   50
   fasten itself to him with every part.
It clasped his belly with its middle claws,
   its forefeet clutched his arms as in a vise,
   and into either cheek it sank its jaws.
The hindmost feet it dug into his thighs,   55
   and twixt them thrust its tail so limberly
   that up his spine its clambering tip could rise.
Never did ivy cling so to a tree
   as did that hideous creature bind and braid
   its limbs and his in pure ferocity;   60
And then they stuck together, as if made
   of melting wax, and mixed their colors; nor
   did either now retain his former shade:
Just so, when paper burns, there runs before
   the creeping flame a stain of darkish hue   65
   that, though not black as yet, is white no more.

The other two cried out to him they knew,
    saying, "Agnello, how you change! Ah me,
    already you are neither one nor two."
The two heads now were one, and we could see   70
    two faces fuse in one blear visage, where
    no vestiges of either seemed to be.
Four forelimbs now combined to make a pair
    of arms, and strange new members grew in place
    of the bellies, legs, and chests that had been there.   75
Their erstwhile shapes were gone without a trace,
    and the monstrous form that was and was not they
    now moved away with slow and stumbling pace.
As lizards, in the cruelest heat of day,
    skitter from hedge to hedge along a lane,   80
    and flash like lightning if they cross the way,
So, toward the bellies of the other twain,
    there sped a little reptile, fiery-hot
    and blackly glinting as a pepper-grain:
It now transfixed, in one of them, the spot   85
    through which our earliest nourishment must come;
    then fell, and sprawled before him like a sot.
The victim gazed at it, and yet was dumb;
    he stood stock-still, and did but yawn a bit,
    as if some drowsy fever made him numb.   90
The serpent looked on him, and he on it;
    from the one's mouth and the other's wound, a spate
    of smoke poured out, and the fumes converged and knit.
Of poor Sabellus' and Nasidius' fate
    let Lucan tell no more, but listen now   95
    to what I saw. Let Ovid not relate
Of Cadmus and of Arethusa, how
    they turned to snake or fountain by his grace;
    no envy of those feats need I avow,
For he never made two creatures, face to face,   100
    so change that each one let the other seize
    its very substance, as in the present case.

Incited by their mutual sympathies,
    the serpent caused its tail now to divide,
    and the wretch pressed together his feet and knees. 105
His legs and thighs adhered then, side to side,
    soon blending so that nowhere, low or high,
    could any seam or juncture be descried.
The cloven tail took on the form that by
    degrees the other lost, and now its skin 110
    turned soft, while the other's hardened in reply.
I saw the armpits of the man begin
    to engulf the arms, while the beast's short forelegs grew
    by just that length to which the arms sank in.
Its two hind feet entwined, and turned into 115
    that member which by mankind is concealed,
    and the thief's one member branched then into two.
Now, while the smoke by which they both were veiled
    transposed their hues, and planted on one crown
    the hair that from the other it plucked and peeled, 120
The one arose, the other toppled down,
    and each, still grimly staring, set about
    to make the other's lineaments his own.
The upright one drew back his upper snout,
    and from his brow the excess matter ran 125
    downward, till from the cheeks two ears grew out;
Then the nether remnant of the snout began,
    out of its superfluity, to make
    a human nose, and the full lips of a man.
The prone one thrust his jaws out like a snake, 130
    and at the same time drew his ears inside,
    as a snail retracts its horns for safety's sake,
And cleft his tongue, that once was unified
    and shaped for speech. Then, in the other's head,
    the forked tongue healed, and the smoke could now subside. 135
The soul that had become a beast now fled
    hissing away; the other, who had begun
    to speak in sputters, followed where it led,

Yet turned his new-made shoulders toward the one
    who lingered, saying, "Buoso shall crawl through this   140
    stony terrain awhile, as I have done."
Thus did the cargo of the seventh abyss
    change and re-change; let the strangeness of it, pray,
    excuse me if my pen has gone amiss.
Although my thoughts were fuddled by dismay   145
    and my eyes a bit uncertain, all the same
    those darkling spirits did not steal away
Ere I knew one for Puccio, called the Lame;
    and he had been the only one to keep
    his form, of the three thieves who earlier came.   150
The other was he, Gaville, who made thee weep.

Florence rejoice, O, you that are so great
    that over sea and over land you beat
    your wings and hell is swollen with your name.
I found among the thieves five citizens
    of yours and the shame of that stays with me   5
    and your honor is not enlarged thereby.
But if we dream the truth as we near morning
    you will now be feeling before long
    what Prato among others prays down on you.
If it were now it would be none too soon.   10
    Since it is sure to happen let it come
    for it will weigh upon me worse with time.
We left that place and up by the stone stair
    of rock ledges that we came down before
    my guide climbed again and drew me after   15
And following the solitary way
    among the rocks and juttings of the cliff
    the foot could not move unless the hand was helping.
Then I felt sorrow and I sorrow now
    when I turn back my mind to what I saw   20
    and more than usually I restrain my genius
Lest it run where Virtue does not guide it,
    so that if favoring star or better thing
    has given me the good I may accept it.
As many fireflies as the peasant resting   25
    on the hill during that season when
    he who gives light to the world hides his face least
At the hour when the fly is yielding to the gnat
    sees down the length of the valley perhaps
    even there where he harvests the grapes and plows   30

With as many flames as that the eighth chasm
   was shining, so it appeared to me when
   I stood where I could look all the way down.
And even as he whom the bears avenged
   beheld Elijah's chariot departing   35
   that time the horses rose straight up to heaven
So that he could not turn his eyes upon
   anything except the flame alone
   like a little cloud in its ascending
Even so, each one moves in the gullet   40
   of the gorge, for in none of them the theft
   appears and every flame palms a sinner.
I had climbed up onto the bridge to look
   and if I had not held on to a rock
   I would have fallen in with none to push me.   45
And the guide, seeing me so rapt,
   said, "Inside those fires are the spirits.
   Each one wraps himself in what burns him."
"My master," I said to him, "hearing you
   has made me sure, but I had already   50
   guessed it was so and was moved to ask you
Who is in that fire that comes divided
   at the top as though it rose from the pyre
   where Eteocles was put beside his brother?"
He answered me: "Inside that one Ulysses   55
   and Diomed suffer and so together
   they endure vengeance as they went in anger
And in their flame they groan for the hiding
   in the horse, which made the doorway for
   the noble seed of the Romans to come through.   60
Inside there they lament the art that has made
   Deidamia even in death mourn for Achilles
   and there they are punished for Palladium."
"If those who are inside the sparks can speak,"
   I said, "I pray you fervently,   65
   and pray again, pray you a thousand times

Not to refuse to allow me to wait
  until the horned flame comes here where we are.
  See how the longing is bending me toward it."
And he to me: "What you pray is worthy   70
  of much praise, and therefore I accept it,
  but you must put a curb on your own tongue.
Leave the speaking to me, for I understand
  what you desire, and it could be that they,
  since they were Greek, might scorn what you would say."   75
After the flame had arrived somewhere that
  seemed to my guide to be the time and place
  this is what I heard him say to it,
"O you that are two within a single fire,
  if I deserved much of you while I lived,   80
  if I deserved of you much or a little
When in the world I wrote the high verses,
  do not move on, but one of you say where
  when he had lost himself he went to die."
The larger horn of the ancient flame   85
  began to shudder, murmuring, the way
  a flame does when the wind harries it.
Then the tip, moving back and forth as though
  it were the tongue that was speaking, flung
  a voice out of itself saying, "When   90
I left Circe who for a year and more
  had held me back, close to Gaeta there,
  before Aeneas gave the place its name
Not affection for my son nor reverence
  for my old father nor that rightful love   95
  that should have brought joy to Penelope
Could subdue the ardor I had in me
  to become experienced in the world
  and in human iniquities and worth,
But I set forth on the open sea   100
  with a single ship and that small company
  that by then had not deserted me.

One shore and the other I saw as far as Spain,
   far as Morocco, the isle of Sardinia
   and the other islands that sea washes round.   105
I and my companions were old and near
   the end when we came to the narrows where
   Hercules set up his warning markers
For men, to tell them they should sail no farther.
   On the right hand I left Seville behind,   110
   on the other I had already left Ceuta.
'O brothers,' I said, 'who through a hundred
   thousand perils have arrived at the west,
   do not deny to the little waking
Time that remains to your senses knowing   115
   for yourselves the world on the far side
   of the sun, that has no people in it.
Consider what you rose from: you were not
   made to live like animals but
   for the pursuit of virtue and knowledge.'   120
With this short speech I so whetted my
   companions for the journey that I
   then could scarcely have held them back
And turning the stern toward the morning we
   made wings of our oars for the insane flight   125
   bearing over the whole time toward the left.
Already the night could see all of the stars
   of the other pole, and ours was so low
   it never rose above the ocean floor.
Five times the light under the moon had been   130
   lighted and as many times put out
   since we had entered on the deep passage
When a mountain appeared dark in the distance
   and it seemed to me that it was higher
   than any I had ever seen before.   135
At the sight we rejoiced, but that turned quickly
   to grief, for out of the new land a whirlwind
   rose that struck the bow of our vessel.

Three times it spun her round with all the waters.
   On the fourth it lifted the stern up   140
   and drove down the prow, as pleased another,
Until the sea was closed over us."

Now the flame burned straight upward and was still
   saying no more, and now from us it
   went with the consent of the gentle poet
When there arrived another from behind it
   that made us turn our eyes to the top of it   5
   toward a confused noise that came out of it.
As the Sicilian bull that bellowed first
   with the moaning (as was no more than just)
   of the one who had tuned it with his file
Bellowed on with the voice of the victim   10
   so that though it was only a brass thing
   it seemed to be transfixed with suffering,
Thus, having from the first no way, no little
   hole out of the fire, the miserable
   words were converted into its language,   15
But after they had taken their journey
   up through the point, giving it those vibrations
   that the tongue had given them on their way,
We heard it say, "O you toward whom I turn
   my voice and who just now were speaking in   20
   Lombard, saying, 'Go now, no more I ask you,'
Though perhaps I have come a little late
   do not be impatient but wait and speak with me.
   See, I am not impatient and I burn.
If you have fallen only now into   25
   this blind world out of that sweet Italian
   land from which all of my guilt I bring
Say have the Romagnoli peace or war
   for I was from the mountains between Urbino there
   and the summit from which the Tiber flows."   30

I was still bent down and listening
   when my guide touched my side, saying,
   "You speak, for this is an Italian."
And I who had my answer ready
   lost no time then but began this way: 35
   "O soul that are hidden under there
Your Romagna is not and never was without
   war in the hearts of its tyrants, though
   none was to be seen now as I left it.
Ravenna is as it has been all these years,   40
   the eagle of Polenta brooding on it
   so that he covers Cervia with his wings.
The city that was put to the long test
   and then made of the French a bleeding hill
   finds itself again under the green claws.   45
Verrucchio's old mastiff and the young one
   who had Montagna in his evil keeping
   are still gnawing at the same places.
The cities of Lamone and Santerno
   are led by the young lion of the white hair   50
   who changes sides from winter to summer
And that city whose flank the Savio washes
   just as it lies between plain and mountain
   so it lives between tyranny and freedom.
Now I pray you to tell us who you are.   55
   Be no harder than one has been toward you,
   so may your name advance still through the world."
After the flame had for a moment roared
   in its own way, the sharp point of it moved
   back and forth, and then gave breath like this: 60
"If I believed that I was answering
   one who would ever go back to the world
   this flame would stand still and shake no further
But since no one ever returned alive
   out of this deep if what I hear is true   65
   without dread of disgrace I answer you.

After a life of arms I turned Franciscan
   thinking, girt with that rope, to make amends
   and my belief would have been fulfilled I am certain
But for the Great Vicar—evil take him—   70
   who set me back into my early sins.
   I would have you hear from me how and why.
While I was the shape of bone and flesh
   my mother gave me, the things I did
   were not those of the lion but the fox.   75
Intricate strategies and covert means
   I knew them all, and used them with such art
   that to the end of the earth the sound went out.
When I saw that I myself had reached
   that part of my age at which everyone   80
   should lower sails and gather the ropes in
What had pleased me before became my grief
   and repenting and confessing I turned friar
   —O, misery—and it would have been enough.
The prince of the new Pharisees, finding   85
   himself at war close to the Lateran
   and not against the Jews or Saracens
For every enemy of his was Christian
   not one of whom had been to conquer Acre
   nor been a merchant in the Sultan's land   90
Regarded neither in himself the highest
   office, his holy orders, nor in me
   that cord that used to make its wearers thin
But as Constantine sought Silvestro on
   Mount Soracte to cure his leprosy   95
   so this one sought me out to be the doctor
Who would cure him of his proud fever,
   asking me for advice and I said nothing
   because his words sounded drunk to me.
And then he said to me, 'Put from your heart any   100
   fear. Here and now I absolve you. Teach me
   how to throw Penestrino to the ground.

Heaven, as you know, I am able
  to close and open. For this are there two keys
  which my predecessor valued little.'   105
I was moved by the weighty arguments
  until I thought silence would be the worst course
  and I said, 'Father, since you wash me
Of this sin into which now I must fall
  be long in promises, short in keeping them,   110
  and you will triumph on the high seat.'
Later, when I was dead, Saint Francis came
  for me but one of the black cherubim
  said, 'Do not take him. Do not do me wrong.
He is bound to come down among my helots   115
  for ever since he gave the fraudulent
  counsel I have had him by the hair
Since none can be absolved without repenting
  nor can repent and want at the same time,
  the contradiction not permitting it.'   120
O, my suffering! How startled I was when
  he seized me saying, 'Maybe you did not
  think that I was a logician.'
He bore me off to Minos and that one curled
  his tail eight times around his hardened back   125
  and then biting it in his great rage
Said, 'This sinner is for the stealing fire,'
  so that here where you see me I am lost
  in this garment, bitter and wandering.''
When he had ended what he had to say   130
  with that, the flame, sorrowing, went its way
  writhing and flinging high its pointed horn.
We continued, I and my guide, along
  the cliff to the next arch which crosses over
  the chasm where the penalty is paid   135
By those whose load comes from cleaving asunder.

Who could find words, even in free-running prose,
   to describe the wounds I saw, in all their horror—
   telling it over as many times as you choose,
It's certain no human tongue could take the measure
   of those enormities. Our speech and mind,   5
   straining to comprehend them, flail, and falter.
If all the Apulians who long ago mourned
   their lives cut off by Trojans could live once more,
   assembled to grieve again with the thousands stained
By their own blood in the long Carthaginian war—   10
   rings pillaged from their corpses poured by the bushel,
   as Livy writes, who never was known to err—
With those who took their mortal blows in battle
   with Robert Guiscard, and those whose bones were heaped
   at Ceperano, killed in the Puglian betrayal,   15
And the soldiers massacred in the stratagem shaped
   by old Alardo, who conquered without a weapon
   near Tagliacozzo when their army was trapped—
And some were showing wounds still hot and open,
   others the gashes where severed limbs had been: 20
   it would be nothing to equal the mutilation
I saw in that Ninth Chasm. No barrel staved-in
   and missing its endpiece ever gaped open as wide
   as the man I saw split open from his chin
Down to the farting-place, and from the splayed   25
   trunk the spilled entrails dangled between his thighs.
   I saw his organs, and the sack that makes the bread
We swallow turn to shit. Seeing my eyes
   fastened upon him, he pulled open his chest
   with both hands, saying, "Look how Maömetto claws   30

And mangles himself, torn open down the breast!
   Look how I tear myself! And Ali goes
   weeping before me—like me, a schismatic, and cleft:
Split open from the chin along his face
   up to the forelock. All you see here, when alive,   35
   taught schism, and so they all are cleavered like this.
A devil waits with a sword back there, to carve
   each of us open afresh each time we've gone
   our circuit around this road, where while we grieve
Our wounds close up before we pass him again—   40
   but who are you that stand here, perhaps to delay
   torments pronounced on your own false words to men?"
"Neither has death yet reached him, nor does he stay
   for punishment of guilt," my master replied,
   "but for experience. And for that purpose I,   45
Who am dead, lead him through Hell as rightful guide,
   from circle to circle. Of this, you can be as sure
   as that I stand and speak to you, here at his side."
More than a hundred shades were gathered there
   who hearing my master's words had halted, and came   50
   along the trench toward me in order to stare,
Forgetting their torment in wonder for a time.
   "Tell Fra Dolcino, you who may see the sun,
   if he wants not to follow soon to the same
Punishment, he had better store up grain   55
   against a winter siege and the snows' duress,
   or the Novarese will easily bring him down"—
After he had lifted his foot to resume the pace,
   Maömetto spoke these words, and having spoken
   he stepped away again on his painful course.   60
Another there, whose face was cruelly broken,
   the throat pierced through, the nose cut off at the brow,
   one ear remaining, stopped and gazed at me, stricken
With recognition as well as wonder. "Ah, you,"
   his bleeding throat spoke, "you here, yet not eternally   65
   doomed here by guilt—unless I'm deceived, I knew

Your face when I still walked above, in Italy.
   If you return to the sweet plain I knew well
   that rises from Marcabò towards Vercelli,
Remember Pier da Medicina. And tell   70
   Sir Guido and Angiolello, two gentlemen
   from Fano: if we have foresight here in Hell
They will be thrown from their own ship to drown
   near La Cattolica by a tyrant's treachery.
   From Cyprus to Majorca, never has Neptune   75
Witnessed such evil in all the history
   of pirates and Argolic raiders. Their betrayer,
   who sees from one eye only (he holds a city
Found bitter by another who's with me here),
   will lure them sailing there for truce-talks—then,   80
   when he has dealt with them, they'll need no prayer
For safe winds near Focara: not ever again."
   Then I to him, "If you'd have me be the bearer
   of news from you to those above, explain—
What man do you mean, who found a city bitter?"   85
   Then he grasped one shade near him by the jaw,
   and opened the mouth, and said, "This is the creature;
He does not speak, who once, in exile, knew
   words to persuade Caesar at the Rubicon
   that hesitation was risky, a treacherous flaw,   90
And: 'Once he's prepared, delaying injures a man.'"
   I saw how helpless Curio's tongue was cut
   to a stub in his throat, whose speech had been so keen.
Then one with both hands lopped off came forward to shout,
   raising the stumps so his cheeks were spattered by blood, 95
   "Remember Mosca Lamberti!—I, too, gave out
Slogans persuading to bloodshed, it was I who said
   'What's done is done with': words that brought such pain
   to the Tuscan people." Then, when he heard me add,
"—and death to your family tree," utterly undone   100
   by sorrow piled on sorrow, the man fell still,
   and walked off like one whom grief has made insane.

I stayed to see more, one sight so incredible
    as I should fear to describe, except that conscience,
    being pure in this, encourages me to tell: 105
I saw—and writing it now, my brain still envisions—
    a headless trunk that walked, in sad promenade
    shuffling the dolorous track with its companions,
And the trunk was carrying the severed head,
    gripping it by the hair like a lantern, letting it swing,   110
    and the head looked up at us: "Oh me!" it cried.
He was himself and his lamp as he strode along,
    two in one, and one in two—and how it can be,
    only He knows, who created every thing.
Reaching the bridge, the trunk held the head up high   115
    so we could hear his words, which were, "Look well,
    you who come breathing to view the dead, and say
If there is a punishment harder than mine in Hell.
    carry the word, and know me: Bertran de Born,
    who made the father and the son rebel   120
The one against the other, by the evil turn
    I did the young king, counseling him to ill.
    David and Absalom had nothing worse to learn
From the wickedness contrived by Achitophel.
    Because I parted their union, I carry my brain   125
    parted from this, its pitiful stem: mark well
This retribution that you see is mine."

The crowds, the dreadful wounds, so filled my eyes
   I stood there staring as if drugged, and all
   I wanted was to stay behind and cry.
But Virgil asked, "What are you looking at?
   Why let your gaze sink down and settle on   5
   the sad dismemberment of souls like that?
You didn't do so at the other ditches.
   Remember—for perhaps you plan to count them—
   twenty-two miles the curving valley stretches.
The moon's already dropped beneath our feet,   10
   the time allotted us is very short,
   many you haven't met remain to meet."
My quick reply was, "If you had inquired
   the reason why I chose to stand there looking,
   you might have let me do as I desired."   15
My guide strode on, while I made haste to follow
   behind, elaborating on my answer
   and adding further, "Deep within that hollow
Which riveted my eyes in a fixed stare,
   one of my relatives, I think, is mourning   20
   the sin that's punished so severely there."
The Teacher said, "From now on do not let
   your thoughts or purpose stray in his direction.
   Set your sights elsewhere; leave him to his fate.
Beneath the little bridge I saw that fellow   25
   pointing his finger at you with a threat,
   and heard them say his name was Geri del Bello.
Your thoughts still caught up with Bertran, the one
   who was the lord of Altaforte, you
   did not catch sight of him, so he moved on."   30

"My noble guide," I said, "the death that came
   to him was murder, yet was not avenged
   by any one of us who shares the shame.
He loathes us all, which was his reason for
   leaving without a word to me, no doubt.   35
   It only makes me pity him the more."
We said this while approaching the first site
   where you could look from cliff-edge to the bottom
   of the next trench, were there sufficient light.
When we'd come up above the last enclosure   40
   of Malebolge, so that its novices
   were visible to us in clear exposure,
My heart was pierced by many a grievous shout,
   the shafts equipped with arrowheads of pity:
   hands covering my ears, I shut them out.   45
The pain resembled what a hospital
   in Valdichiana, from July to September
   (Maremma, too, Sardinia as well),
Might house, but gathered in a single trench.
   It was like that; and, pouring forth, as though   50
   from limbs with gangrene, came a horrible stench.
We made our way down to the farthest edge
   of the long cliff, still bearing to the left,
   the vista clearer now, so sight could dredge
Those lower depths, down where the minister   55
   of the Most High, unerring Justice herself,
   corrects the forgers she takes note of here.
I doubt that all the scourged inhabitants
   of Aegina were more a wretched sight,
   the day its air filled with such evil taints   60
That every creature, even small worms, too,
   succumbed—and afterward a second people
   (tradition tells, which poets hold as true)
Were reborn from the race of ants—than met
   our eyes in that dark valley where those sluggish   65
   spirits in random heaps repaid their debt.

This one would lie on top another's back,
  that one on another's belly, and some
  crawled on all fours along the dismal track.
We moved on without haste and didn't speak,   70
  observing, overhearing the afflicted,
  who couldn't stand upright they were so weak.
Leaning against each other, I saw two
  of them propped like saucepans being warmed,
  spotted with sores and scabs from head to toe.   75
I never saw a stableboy, at work
  with currycomb for an impatient master,
  or someone kept against his will awake,
Apply as hard as these men did the scrape
  of nails on flesh to ease that savage itching   80
  from which there otherwise was no escape.
And so the scabs were raked off by their nails,
  much as a cleaning knife is used on bream
  or other fish possessed of larger scales.
"You, unraveling your own skin with your fingers,"   85
  began my guide to one of them, "yes, you,
  who sometimes use them like a pair of pincers,
Say whether among those with you there might be
  any Italians—and may your nails
  last out their work for all eternity."   90
"We two you see here ravaged with disease
  are Italians both," said one of them in tears.
  "But who are you who've made these inquiries?"
And my guide said: "A spirit willing to climb
  down here from ledge to ledge with this live man,   95
  so I might show the lower world to him."
They broke off propping up each other, and
  both of them shuddered as they turned my way
  along with some who'd heard at second hand.
My thorough teacher came in close to me   100
  and said, "Now tell them what you want to hear."
  Thus I began, obeying his decree:

"So that your story may not be withdrawn
    from human memory in the world above,
    but live again beneath another sun,   105
Say who you are, and give your people's name.
    Don't let your gruesome punishment stop you
    from speaking out because you fear the shame."
"I was from Arezzo," one of them replied,
    "burned at the stake by Albero of Siena.   110
    But why I'm punished here is not why I died.
It's true that—as a joke—I told him once
    I could rise and fly up in the air.
    And he, who had more eagerness than sense,
Begged me to teach him; but I couldn't make   115
    a Daedalus of him, and so he asked
    his godfather to burn me at the stake.
But Minos, whose strong judgments cannot err,
    condemned me to the last of these ten ditches
    because I practiced alchemy up there."   120
I said to the poet, "Has there ever been
    a people sillier than the Siennese?
    Even the French are more substantial men."
And then the other leper, hearing me,
    answered my comment, "Ah, except for Stricca,   125
    who mastered the art of spending prudently,
And Niccolò, the very first to know
    how to make use of high-priced cloves, inside
    that garden plot where suchlike seeds may grow;
Excepting, too, those in whose company   130
    Caccia d'Ascian sold off his woods and vineyards,
    and 'Spellbound' handed out his wisdom free.
But so you may know who's of the same mind
    as you about the Siennese, look closer
    at this face, which will answer you in kind: 135
You see the spirit of Cappocchio here,
    who transmuted metals by alchemy;
    you'll remember, if you're who I think you are,
How close my copies came to reality."

CANTO XXX / *Alfred Corn*

The time when Juno, told of Semele,
    became enraged (as she had more than once)
    against the Theban royal family,
King Athamas went mad, and in that plight,
    seeing his wife approach burdened with one   5
    son on her left arm and one on her right,
Shouted: "Cast forth the nets so I may catch
    the lioness and her cubs as they go by."
    He reached with merciless talons to snatch
The first, whose name was Learchus, then spun   10
    him in the air and dashed him against a rock.
    His wife drowned herself with the other son.
And after Fortune's turning wheel brought low
    the majesty of Troy, which risked its all,
    king and kingdom crushed with the same blow,   15
Hecuba—captive, grieving all the more
    after she saw Polyxena was dead
    and heard that Polydorus, cast ashore
By the waves, was another loss to mourn—
    began to bark as though she were a dog,   20
    her mind undone by sufferings she had borne.
But Furies whether Theban or from Troy
    were never seen to strike dumb beasts or human
    limbs so hard as those I saw deploy
Their skills in two souls there, stripped naked, pale,   25
    who ran and tore the others' flesh like swine
    set loose from pigsties that had been their jail.
One reached Capocchio and sank sharp teeth
    into his nape, then dragged him forward so
    his belly scraped the hard-packed earth beneath.   30

The man from Arezzo remained, and, trembling, said,
  "That goblin's Gianni Schicchi; he runs about
  like a mad dog and 'grooms' the other dead."
"O," I said, "may the second one not tear
  your back with his fangs, but will you kindly tell me   35
  who it is, before it speeds from here."
"That is the old spirit," he said to me,
  "of scandalous Myrrha, one whose love for her
  father defied the bounds of decency.
She got to sin with him as she wanted to   40
  by taking on the appearance of someone else—
  just like that first one going off now, who,
Coveting the best of the old man's mules,
  dared to impersonate Buoso Donati
  and draft his will according to the rules."   45
As soon as those two mad dogs left, the ones
  I had been staring at intently, I turned
  around to look at other ill-starred sons.
I saw one who, had his thin legs been cut
  off at the groin, where limbs meet in a fork,   50
  would be the very image of a lute.
Dropsy, which puts awry the human body
  because of fluids it cannot absorb
  (so that the head's too small to match the belly),
Forced his mouth to gape, as though he burned   55
  with fever and a thirst that made one lip
  stretch downward, while the other upward turned.
He said to us, "You men who though in Hell
  seem not to suffer punishment (I don't
  know how) behold then, and consider well,   60
Master Adam's downfall. When alive
  I mostly got what I wanted: now, alas!
  A single drop of water's all I crave.
From the Casentino's verdant hill
  country, brooklets flow down into the Arno,   65
  making their winding channels moist and chill:

I'm forced to see them now, in this grim place,
    because their image sears me even more
    than the affliction that distorts my face.
Unyielding Justice who chastises me   70
    uses the very spot where I once sinned
    to make me sigh and groan more frequently.
There is Romena, where I managed to fake
    the seal of John the Baptist on a coin,
    for which, up there, they burned me at the stake.   75
Were I to see the sad ghosts here tonight
    of Guido, Alessandro, or their brother—
    for Branda Springs I'd not exchange the sight.
These spirits milling around like stirred-up dregs
    pretend that one of them's already here.   80
    But does that help a man with useless legs?
I would already, were my body no
    more agile than to crawl each hundred years
    an inch, have started on the path; I'd go
Looking for him among those marred with loss   85
    of limbs, though the trench curves eleven miles
    around and measures fully half across.
Because of them I'm added to this family:
    they had me counterfeit a florin cast
    with about three carats of impurity."   90
Then I asked, "Who are those two foolish souls
    that steam like wet hands bared to winter cold
    and lie together next your right-hand walls?"
He said, "I found them here—and not since then
    have they stirred—when I first rained into this ditch,   95
    nor do I think they'll ever move again.
The first is she who slandered Joseph, the other,
    lying Sinon, the Trojan Greek: their high
    fever gives off that stench in which we smother."
One of them, enraged at being dismissed   100
    in such a dim description, reached to strike
    the speaker's swollen belly with his fist.

The tight skin boomed as though it were a drum:
    then Master Adam hit him in the face,
    using what looked like quite a hard forearm,   105
And said to him: "Although mobility
    has been taken from my heavy limbs,
    for jobs like this I still have an arm free."
To which he answered: "The day you went to join
    the flames, your arm was not as swift, but it   110
    was that and more when you were forging coin."
The man with dropsy said, "That much is true,
    but as a witness you were not so truthful
    when those at Troy requested truth from you."
"If I spoke falsely, you still counterfeited,"   115
    said Sinon, "and I'm here for one sin only.
    You, for more than any fiend's committed!"
The one who had the swollen belly said,
    "Perjurer! May the memory of the horse and
    that all men know your crime fill you with dread."   120
"May thirst fill *you* with dread," the Greek replies,
    "as your tongue cracks and filthy water bloats
    your paunch into a hedge before your eyes."
And then the coiner: "As usual, your mouth
    hangs open because you're sick; but even though   125
    I suffer thirst and dropsy puffs me out,
Your head aches, and your body is on fire,
    so that, to go and lick Narcissus' mirror,
    two words of invitation's all you'd require."
Intent on them, I stood there like a stone   130
    until my master said, "I'm going to
    be harsh with you if this does not end soon!"
But when I felt his wrath addressed to me,
    I turned to him with shame so great that even
    now it revolves within my memory.   135
Like one who dreams his own misfortune, who
    while dreaming wishes he were only dreaming
    and craves what is as though it were not so,

Thus I became aware I'd lost the use
    of speech from trying to excuse myself,   140
    not seeing muteness made its own excuse.
The master said, "Much less shame might atone
    for greater misdeeds than yours was, therefore,
    whatever remorse you feel you may disown.
Remember, I am always there with you   145
    should circumstances ever send you among
    people engaged in like disputes, for to
Give them your attention is base and wrong."

CANTO XXXI / *Sharon Olds*

The same tongue first stung me
    staining me on both cheeks
    and then offered me the remedy.
So I have heard the lance of Achilles
    and his father would be the instrument   5
    first of a painful and then a welcome gift.
We turned our backs on the wretched valley,
    went up the bank that encloses it
    and crossed over without another word.
Here it was less than night and less than day   10
    so I could see only a little way ahead
    but I heard the sound of a horn so loud
It would have made any thunder seem faint
    and it drew my eyes, which followed its course
    backward, to one spot.   15
After the bitter defeat when Charlemagne
    lost his sacred company
    Roland did not blow as rendingly.
I had not been staring at that spot long
    when I thought I saw many high towers   20
    so I asked, "Master, tell me, what city is that?"
And he said to me, "Since you are trying to pierce
    the dark from too far off
    your imagination has misled you.
You will easily see if you get there   25
    how much our eyes are deceived by distance
    so spur yourself forward."
Then he took me tenderly by the hand
    and said, "Before we go any further
    so that the fact will seem less strange to you   30

Let me tell you those are not towers but giants
    standing in a pit, from the waist down
    they are all inside its bank."
As, when fog is dispersing, one's gaze
    little by little puts together   35
    what the vapor that thickened the air concealed
So as I penetrated the heavy darkness
    and came closer and closer to the brink
    error fled, and fear grew in me.
As on its circular wall   40
    Montereggione crowns itself with towers
    so do the upper bodies of horrible giants
Turret the bank which encircles the pit,
    the ones whom Jove still menaces
    from the heavens when he thunders.   45
I could already discern the face of one of them,
    the shoulders and chest and much
    of the belly and his arms along his sides.
When nature gave up the art of making
    creatures like these she did well   50
    depriving Mars of such enforcers.
And if she does not repent of making elephants
    and whales, anyone who considers this carefully
    will find her all the more just and prudent,
For when the agency of a mind   55
    is joined to ill will and to power
    we cannot defend ourselves.
His face seemed to me as long and broad
    as the pine cone at St. Peter's in Rome
    and his other bones were in proportion   60
So that the bank which aproned him
    from the waist down showed so much above it
    that three Frisians would have boasted falsely
That they could reach his hair.
    I saw thirty great spans of him   65
    down from where a man buckles his cloak.

"Raphel may amech zabi almi,"
   his fierce mouth, for which sweeter psalms
   were not suited, began to shriek.
And my guide said to him, "Stupid spirit,   70
   stick to your horn and use it as a vent
   when rage or other passions touch you.
Feel at your neck and you will find the strap
   that holds it tied, O muddled soul,
   what did you think that was curving across your chest?"   75
Then he said to me, "He is his own accuser.
   This is Nimrod, because of whose evil thoughts
   a common language is not used on earth.
Let us leave him here and not talk uselessly,
   for every language is to him   80
   as his to others, understood by no one."
We made our way farther, bearing left
   and at the distance of a crossbow shot
   we found the next giant, larger and more savage.
Who the master was who had bound him   85
   I do not know, but his left arm was shackled
   in front of him and his right behind
By a chain which entwined him from the neck down
   so that where he was uncovered
   it was wound to the fifth coil.   90
"This proud spirit wanted to test the power
   of his strength against great Jove,"
   said my guide, "and he received this reward.
His name is Ephialtes, and he made his bold attempts
   at the time when the giants terrorized the gods.   95
   The arms he lifted he will never move again."
And I said to him, "If it were possible
   I would wish that my eyes could experience
   the immense Briareus."
And he answered, "Near here you will see   100
   Antaeus, who can speak and is not chained
   and who will set us down at the bottom of all guilt.

The one you wish to see is much farther on,
    he is shackled and fashioned like this one
    except that his face looks more ferocious."   105
No great earthquake ever shook
    a tower as violently
    as Ephialtes suddenly shook himself.
Then more than ever I feared I might die
    and fright alone would have killed me   110
    if I had not seen his restraints.
We went farther on and came
    to Antaeus, who stuck up out of the pit
    a good five ells, not counting his head.
"O you who, in the fateful valley   115
    which made Scipio the heir of glory
    when Hannibal and his men showed him their backs,
Once took a thousand lions as spoils
    and who, had you stayed in the high war
    with your brothers, some still believe, could have helped   120
Bring those sons of earth to victory,
    set us below, and do not scorn the task,
    down there where the cold locks Cocytus.
Do not make us ask Tityus or Typhon.
    This man can give what you long for here   125
    so reach down, and take that sneer off your face.
He can still restore your fame in the world.
    He is alive, and expects to live a long time
    if grace does not call him back early."
So my master spoke and the other hastily   130
    held out his hands, whose huge squeeze
    Hercules had felt, and took up my guide.
Virgil, when he felt himself taken up,
    said to me, "Come here, so I can take you."
    Then he made one bundle of himself and me.   135
As the Garisenda seems when you look up along
    the underside of its slant, when a cloud is passing over
    against the direction of its tilt,

So, as I waited and watched, Antaeus seemed to me
   when he stooped over us, at that moment   140
   I wished I had gone by some other way
But lightly onto the deep which swallows
   Lucifer with Judas he set us down,
   nor did he stay leaning in that place
And like the mast of a ship he lifted up.   145

CANTO XXXII / *Deborah Digges*

Were there a language dark enough to speak
   truly of that hole harrowed by crags
   gravity itself could not fall through to,
I could taste the salt of my conception.
   But words are abstract, sadly approximate,   5
   dull with use. I'm afraid to move my mouth,
Afraid to shape sounds which might conjure
   the bottom of the universe, mouth which once
   knew no more than the sweet suck of *mama,*
Papa. May the voices the stones followed down   10
   the mountain all the way to Thebes find me
   as they found Amphion's lyre, here bear witness.
—Hopeless beyond reason, O disfigured crowds
   in the place where words fail me, better you
   had grazed mindlessly as goats or sheep—.   15
When we had reached the well's floor below
   the Giants' feet, and lower yet down the slope,
   I still gazed behind me at the high wall.
Then I heard a voice call out to me,
   "Watch where you step. Watch you don't kick   20
   the heads of your miserable brothers."
And as I turned I saw a lake of ice,
   stone solid, suffocating smooth,
   as far from its source as glass from sand.
The Danube where it descends to Austria   25
   freezes all the way across, just as the Don's
   wide, snow-swirling surface swallows the sky.
Yet water scores the bedrock underneath.
   But here, had Tambernic and Pietrapana's
   mountains crashed down upon it, it would not give.   30

And as a bullfrog croaks, its head tipped above
   the pond where the poor, remembering, pale
   at their desires, or flush in shame,
So, stuck in the ice, such shades, the heads
   held fast, their teeth clicking like a stork's   35
   desperate beating against a marsh's
Early freeze. None would look up at me,
   but I could see by their mouths how they suffered
   the cold, by their eyes how their hearts grieved.
I took them in. And then near to my feet   40
   I saw two who must have been pressed so long
   this way, face to face, their hair seemed of one
Head. "You," I said to them joined at the breast,
   "who are you?" They lay their heads back and gazed
   at me and strained again upright as if to speak.   45
But their eyes began to tear and the tears
   which had once fallen freely, wetting their faces,
   now locked their lips and sealed their eyelids
Shut. No clamp ever welded beam to beam
   so seamlessly, and they butted their heads   50
   like rams, one crossing the other's mountain.
And another who had lost his ears to the cold
   and kept his head down, perhaps to protect
   his eyes, berated me: "Why do you stare
At us? If you want to know who they are,   55
   they might have shared Bisenzio's valley.
   Alberto was their father. Yes, they are
Born of the same mother. Look around you.
   In all of Caina you will not find two
   brothers more fit to be embraced by this ice.   60
Not the traitor whom Arthur killed. They say
   you could see daylight through the wound,
   Mordred's own shadow brightening. No, not Focaccia
Either. Nor even this one here who blocks
   my view. His name was Sassol Mascheroni.   65
   Are you a Tuscan?—You would know him . . ."

And then, "I'm tired of talking. Leave me alone."
  And then his name, "Camicion de'Pazzi.
  I am waiting for Carlino. Next to him
My sins are nothing. . . ." When I looked up again   70
  I saw the thousand doglike faces, lips blue
  from the cold, and I shuddered, as I always
Will when I survey a lake, a pond, part
  of a river frozen. So we approached
  that center, and I still shivered in the eternal   75
Shade, a little behind my Guide. And whether
  I willed it, or did so by chance, or fate,
  my foot struck hard one of those faces
So that it began to weep, "Why kick me?
  Unless you come to avenge Montaperti,   80
  why do you kick me so, why torment me?"
I turned to my Master. "Wait for me,"
  I said, and in saying heard how anger distracts
  fear. "I have a question for this one."
And I was glad to see my Master stop   85
  with me among those heads, and to the one
  still cursing bitterly I asked, "Why do you
Insult us?" "Why do *you* go carelessly
  through Antenora kicking us?" he replied.
  "If you were alive your boot could not kick   90
Harder . . ." "I *am* alive." I knelt beside him.
  "I could give you something after all. Tell me
  your name. I'll write it down among the others . . ."
"Go away," was his answer. "I want nothing
  from you. Go away and stop harassing me.   95
  Your flattery is useless in this valley."
At that I grabbed him by the scruff like a dog.
  "Tell me your name," I said. "Tell me or you
  will not have even a hair left on your head."
"So snatch me bald," he taunted. "Go on. I swear   100
  I will not tell you my name, nor show you
  my face. Go on. Pound my head a thousand times."

My hands still tangled in his hair, I pulled out
   yet another fistful while he howled
   but he would not say the name or show his face,   105
Even as another head close by called, "Bocca,
   why do you sing so? What devil is in you?
   Bad enough we overhear you mumbling—
Must you bark too?" "A-ha! Say nothing more—
   I know your name!" I cried. "I'll carry back   110
   a true report of you, *Bocca* . . ." "Go away,"
He repeated. "Tell any story you
   see fit, if you make it back at all. But
   don't overlook *that* pretty one, him with the tongue
So ready, just now, to betray me. *He* grieves   115
   a Frenchman's silver. Yes, report it this way:
   'Buoso da Duera freezes with sinners . . .'
And if you're asked the names of others here,
   the one beside you is called Beccheria.
   Florence saw his throat slit for his 'loyalties . . .'   120
There's Gianni de' Soldanier a little
   farther down the slope with Ganelon, and
   Tebaldello, traitor to the Ghibelline refugees—
He opened Faenza's gates at dawn. . . ." We had
   walked on. He still called after us as we   125
   approached two frozen in a single hole, one
Head a helmet for the other. There,
   as a starving man forgets himself, one—
   teeth inside the vault—gnawed the other's brain
Just as Tydeus once gnawed Menalippus'   130
   temples. With no less bloody pleasure did
   this one chew at skull, tendons, arteries.
"You there," I pleaded. I was undone, arrested—
   "Why do you devour him? Tell me the cause.
   If we agree his sins deserve this bestial   135
Punishment, I, knowing who you are,
   and knowing his crimes against you, will speak
   of you on earth, if my tongue doesn't wither."

He lifted his mouth up from the savage feast,
   that sinner, and wiped his lips on the hair
   of the head he'd been gnawing at the back of.
Then began: "You want me to call up
   sorrow so desperate that the thought of it   5
   wrings my heart before my tongue can speak.
But if my words bear seed of infamous fruit
   for this traitor I've set my teeth into,
   then you will see me speak and weep together.
I don't know who you are or how you came   10
   to be down here; but I would guess
   from your accent that you must be Florentine.
I was, as you should know, Count Ugolino
   and this is the Archbishop Ruggieiri.
   I'll tell you why we came to be such neighbors.   15
How, because of his evil schemes, I,
   who trusted him, was taken prisoner
   and killed, I do not need to tell you.
But what you can't have heard, the cruel death
   this beast devised for me, you'll hear now—   20
   then you tell me if I've been wronged.
There was a narrow hole in the prison wall—
   because of me it is called the Hunger Tower;
   other men are going to be imprisoned there—
And I'd already watched moon after moon   25
   through its opening when I dreamed the evil dream
   that for me tore the veil from the future.
There was a hunt—this man appeared as lord
   and master, chasing down a wolf with whelps
   in the mountains between Lucca and Pisa.   30

He had set the Gualandi out in front
   to flush his prey, with Sismondi and Lafranchi,
   and his trained hounds, lean and hungry.
And after a short run it seemed to me
   the father-wolf and his sons were badly tired;   35
   I seemed to see sharp teeth ripping at their flanks.
I woke before the sun came up and heard
   my sons, who were shut in with me there,
   crying in their sleep, asking for bread.
You are cruel if it doesn't make you grieve,   40
   thinking what my heart forewarned me of.
   If you don't weep now, what would make you weep?
The boys had awakened—it was about the time
   when food was usually brought in to us
   and each of us was anxious from his dream—   45
And I heard them then nailing shut the door
   of that awful tower. I looked into the faces
   of my sons, and couldn't speak a word.
I didn't weep. I turned to stone inside.
   They wept. 'You look so strange, Father,'   50
   my little Anselmo said. 'Is something wrong?'
Still I didn't cry. I didn't say a word
   to them that day, or all through the night,
   not till the next sun came into the world.
When a little ray of light had made its way   55
   into our sad prison, I saw four faces,
   each with a look they must have seen on mine.
I bit into my hands from grief.
   And they, thinking I had done it from the need
   to eat, jumped up quickly, saying,   60
'Father, we would find it far less painful
   if you ate of us; it was you who dressed us
   in this miserable flesh: now take it off.'
I calmed myself then to spare them worse sadness.
   We were completely silent that day and the next.   65
   Ah, hard earth! Why did you not open?

When we had come into the fourth day,
 Gaddo threw himself full length at my feet,
 and cried out, 'Father, why don't you help me?'
And died. Then, just as you see me here,   70
 I saw the other three fall one by one
 between the fifth and sixth day, and I,
Already blind, kept crawling over them,
 calling their names for two days after they were dead.
 Then hunger did to me what grief could not."   75
And when he said this, his eyes flaring,
 he sank his teeth into that wretched skull
 And held on, as strong as a dog on a bone.
Ah, Pisa, disgrace to all the peoples
 of this sweet land where the *si* is spoken,   80
 since your neighbors are so slow to punish you,
May Capraia and Gorgona swim
 into the Arno's mouth and dam it up
 and drown every soul inside of you!
Because even though Count Ugolino   85
 betrayed some of your castles, you should never
 have put his children to such torture.
Their young years declare the innocence—
 you younger Thebes!—of Uguiccione and Brigata
 and the other two boys my song has named.   90
We passed on farther, to a place where the ice
 held another sort of folk in its harsh grip,
 not bent over, but with their heads thrown back.
The very weeping there prevents all weeping,
 and grief, which finds no outlet at the eye,   95
 turns inward to increase the anguish—
Because the first tear, as it gathers,
 freezes in the well of the eye and gives
 the face the aspect of a crystal mask.
Though my own face was as numb as a callus   100
 from the cold, as if all feeling had fled
 to look for shelter in some other place,

I thought I felt the stirring of a wind
 and said, "Master, how can this be? Isn't
 all movement of the air down here exhausted?"   105
And he to me: "We'll be in a place soon
 where you can see for yourself what it is
 that drives these winds down from above."
And one of the wretches in the frozen crust
 cried out to us, "You, souls wicked enough   110
 to have been assigned to this last place,
Pluck these hard veils, I pray you, from my eyes
 so I can ease the pain that swells my heart,
 just a little, before my tears freeze again."
So I said to him: "If you want my help,   115
 tell me who you are, and if I fail you,
 may I be banished to the depths of the ice."
He answered, "I am Friar Alberigo,
 the one of the garden of evil fruit,
 who gets paid back here dates for figs."   120
"What!" I cried. "Then you're already dead?"
 "How my body is faring in the world above,"
 he answered, "I have no way of knowing.
This Ptolomea is a place so privileged
 that oftentimes a soul will fall down here   125
 even before Atropos has let it go.
And so that you'll be more willing to clear
 these tears of glass from my eyes, I'll tell you
 now that when a soul commits treachery
As I did, its body is taken from it   130
 by a demon who lives in it and rules it
 until all its time on earth is done.
The soul falls headlong into this cistern;
 up above, meanwhile, the body, like the soul's
 wintering behind me here, still walks about.   135
You must know him, if you've just come down.
 He is Ser Branca d'Oria, and many years
 have gone by since he was frozen in."

"I believe," I said, "that you are lying,
   because Branca d'Oria is not dead—   140
   he eats and drinks and sleeps and puts on clothes."
"Michel Zanche had not yet been mired
   in the ditch of Malebranch," he said, "the place
   above us where the black tar boils,
When this fellow left his body to a devil.   145
   One of his kinsmen did the same, the one
   who helped him carry off the perfidy.
But we've said enough. Reach your hand in here
   and clear my eyes." I didn't clear his eyes.
   It was good manners to treat the villain badly.   150
O you Genoese, who are strangers
   to all good custom, who teem with every vice,
   why hasn't the world erased you altogether?
Look: beside the most wicked spirit in Romagna
   I have found this countryman of yours,   155
   and his soul is bathed in Cocytus
Though his body is alive and walks the earth.

CANTO XXXIV / *Robert Hass*

"Those are the banners of the King of Hell
   in front of us, so keep your eyes open,"
   my master said, "and see if you can see him."
As if at a distance in heavy fog
   or through the dim twilight in our hemisphere   5
   one saw a windmill slowly turning,
I saw some kind of building looming there;
   but the wind was so strong I hid, as I could,
   behind him; there was no other shelter.
I was now (with fear I put it down in verse)   10
   in a place where the shades are sheathed in ice
   and show through like flecks of straw in glass.
Some are lying down, some standing straight,
   this one with his head up, that one his feet;
   another, head bent to heels, like a bow.   15
When we had gone ahead again some way,
   my master seemed to think it time to show me
   that creature who was once so beautiful.
He stepped from in front of me and stopped.
   "Behold Dis," he said, "and behold a place   20
   where you will need to put your courage on."
How I froze at that moment, how weak I felt,
   reader, don't ask. I'm not going to write it.
   And could not if I would: the words would fail.
I did not die, and yet I was not alive—   25
   imagine for yourself, if you have wit,
   what I was then, having neither life nor death.
The emperor of that dolorous kingdom
   rose up from the ice to about mid-chest;
   I am something nearer to a giant in size   30

Than a giant is to one of his arms;
    from such proportions you can estimate,
    going from part to whole, how huge he was.
If, when he raised his brow against his maker,
    he was as beautiful as he is ugly now,   35
    all sorrow must indeed proceed from him.
Oh, what a great marvel it was to me
    when I saw there were three faces in his head!
    There was one in front, and it was scarlet;
The other two, which adjoined the first   40
    just above the middle of the shoulder,
    met at the top of the head to form a crest:
The right face seemed a whitish-yellow color;
    the one on the left had the look of those people
    who come from the land the Nile flows out of.   45
Beneath each face unfurled two huge wings,
    of sufficient size to carry such a bird:
    I never saw sails at sea so broad.
They had no feathers, but were like a bat's
    in texture, and when he flapped them,   50
    he created the three prodigious winds
With which all Cocytus was frozen hard.
    He wept from six eyes, and down his three chins
    tears dripped, and a lot of bloody foam.
In each mouth his teeth chawed on one sinner,   55
    as if he were grinding stalks of flax,
    and thus he tortured three of them at once.
For the one in front the biting was nothing
    compared to the clawing, which stripped his back
    sometimes of every single shred of skin.   60
"That soul up there who gets the worst punishment,"
    my master said, "is Judas Iscariot,
    with his head in the mouth and legs flailing.
Of the other two whose heads are hanging down,
    that's Brutus dangling from the black muzzle—   65
    see how he writhes and doesn't say a word;

The other, who looks so sinewy, is Cassius.
   But night is rising again, and it is time
   for us to go; we have seen everything."
As he directed, I clasped him round the neck,   70
   and taking his chances from the time and place,
   when the great wings were wide enough apart,
He grabbed at the hairy flanks and held;
   and then began his descent tuft by tuft
   between the matted pelt and the frozen crust.   75
When we had come to the place where the thigh
   joins the swelling of the hip, my guide, straining,
   breathing hard, worked himself carefully around
So that his head was where his feet had been,
   and then he clutched at the hair as if to climb.   80
   I thought that we were going back toward Hell.
"Hold on tight," my master said, panting
   from exhaustion, "for these are the stairs
   by which we'll take our leave of so much evil."
He climbed out through a crevice in the rock,   85
   let me off on the rim where I could sit,
   and pulled himself nimbly up beside me.
I lifted my eyes—I thought that I would see
   Lucifer as we had left him; instead
   I saw his legs towering above me.   90
Common folk, who wouldn't understand
   what point it was I'd just passed through,
   could best imagine my perplexity.
"Get up," the master said, "onto your feet.
   The way is long and the road is arduous—   95
   and the sun's already well up in the sky."
It was no palace hall we'd come into,
   but a kind of natural dungeon
   with rough-hewn floors and very little light.
"Before I pull myself up from this abyss,   100
   Master," I said when I was standing again,
   "say a word and clear up my confusion.

Where is the ice? And why is he fixed there
   upside down? And how is it that the sun
   has run so swiftly from evening to morning?"   105
"You still suppose we're on the other side
   of the center," he said, "where I grasped the hair
   of this evil worm the world is pierced by.
Going down, you were on the other side.
   When I turned around, you passed through the point   110
   toward which all weight in the world is drawn.
Now you're beneath the celestial hemisphere,
   exactly opposite the great dry land
   under whose highest point the man was killed
Who was born and lived without sin.   115
   Just here you are standing on the little sphere
   that forms the other face of the Judecca.
And here it's morning when it's evening there.
   And this one, whose pelt we used as a ladder,
   is fixed in the ice as he was before.   120
It was on this side that he fell from Heaven;
   the land that was here veiled itself in the sea
   and fled from its place in fear of him
And came into our hemisphere; perhaps
   whatever stuff was here also fled him   125
   and made this hollow space as it rushed upward."
There is down there at the cave's far end,
   at the point farthest from Beelzebub,
   a place not known by sight, but by the sound
Of a little stream that descends there,   130
   down an easy slope, through a tunnel in the rock
   it has worn away in its winding course.
My guide and I set out on that hidden path
   to make our way into the bright world again,
   and so we climbed with no thought of rest—   135
He first and I second—until we reached ground
   where I could see through a rounded opening
   the night sky with the beautiful things it carries;
And we came out and looked up at the stars.

AFTERWORD

Dante's Style

D ANTE HAS LONG BEEN a vital part of the American spiritual and poetic landscape, and from all signs it is unlikely that interest in him will decline in the immediate future. If anything, this collaborative volume of translations of the *Inferno* shows that Dante continues to be such an inspiring source for the cultivation of contemporary American mythmakers that he increasingly comes forth as nothing less than the quintessentially American phenomenon of a poetic "founding father."

In antiquity the encomiasts as well as the critics of Homer, who were both equally under his powerful spell, believed that he should (or, as the case may be, lamented that he did) occupy a special status in Greek society because he was the educator of Hellas. Homer was variously revered or attacked because he was esteemed to be the rhapsodist of common memories that preserved the ethos of Greece's archaic past and, arguably by the same token, stifled the possibility of the future.

Antiquity's cult of Homer, roughly speaking, describes present-day general reaction to Dante in Italy. As it happened with Homer in the days of Plato, Dante is acknowledged in Italy as if he were the institutional custodian of the ethos of the past; the *Divine Comedy*, just as the *Odyssey* in ancient Greece, is the central ingredient in the school curriculum, a sort of untouchable, semisacred encyclopedia for the education of the soul of young people; various cantos from the *Divine Comedy* are formally (and forcefully) spoon-fed to the young; Dante's own superior genius among poets is quickly accepted as inimitable, and the recognition is an overt alibi to evade the challenge of confronting the demands of his poetry. But in America the fascination with Dante belongs to a different and more complex order of experience.

Because this fascination goes back to the early nineteenth century and it also involves English Romantic poets (for example, Shelley's *Triumph of Life*), it is possible to guess that the common passion for Dante is primarily an allegorical cipher for a romantic fascination with imagination's freedom and sublime inventions. As the maker of new worlds, as the prophet who never blunts the edge of what he says, as the moralist who offers a pattern for the construction of justice in Everyman's soul, as the visionary who makes available a vast range of experiences, Dante comes to stand for the nineteenth-century Romantics as the very archpoet of modernity.

Emerson, on the other hand, who translated into English the *Vita Nuova*, saw in Dante neither simply an abstract image of poetry nor the pretext for the idolatry of the glories of the past. On the strength of his belief that all thoughts cannot exist apart from experiences, Emerson was bound to view the *Divine Comedy* as the empirical model for the future figuration of what he perceived as the extraordinariness of the American experience. The new world of the *Divine Comedy* that Dante had envisioned became for him the prefiguration of a poetic model for the New World. What the "eye of Dante" saw in his journeyings into the realm of the imagination, Emerson mused in a number of his journal entries, would always remain a mystery. But a clue to this mystery was Dante's bold forcing of tumultuous, contradictory experiences of reality within a unitary encyclopedic vision.

The power of Emerson's utterances decisively shaped the future of Dante's presence in American poetry, and they exercised an incalculable influence on the direction of Dante studies in the academic circles of America. The Dante Society of America, which was founded in Cambridge in 1881, became the forum for proselytizing for Dante. At Cambridge Longfellow, Norton, and Russell Lowell are the three major critical interpreters of Dante's poetry and thought, and of the three it is Longfellow, the translator of the *Divine Comedy* into English, who marks a shift to an understanding of Dante in a historical context.

If Emerson had generously focused on the power of Dante's vision to enlarge our moral sympathies, to produce an insight into the organization of the whole of life that would otherwise be unavailable to prosaic intellects, and to make us penetrate to the heart of that totality, Longfellow directs our attention to the ways in which Dante's poem provides textual crystallizations of Emerson's brilliant generalities. What Emerson saw as the grand construction of Dante's utopian imagination, Longfellow locates in the linguistic theories Dante articulated in his *De Vulgari Eloquentia* and in the array of styles he deploys in the *Divine Comedy*.

In the unfinished two books of his *De Vulgari Eloquentia* Dante reflects, first, on the metaphysics of language. Language, we are told, is a divine gift man received in the Garden of Eden; the Edenic unity of language was erased by man's fall, which in turn engendered the confusion of tongues at the Tower of Babel and, later, the Incarnation of the Word as the redemptive event of history's linguistic chaos. Within this over-arching scheme of creation in terms of language, Dante focuses on the fragmentary linguistic geography of Italy and puts forth a view of language capable of expressing the poetic, legal, political, and moral realities of the country. In book two of this treatise, on the other hand, Dante turns his attention to poetry and its technical-rhetorical issues, such as rhythm, metrical patterns, feminine rhymes (which are accented on the penultimate syllable), subdivisions of stanzas, the aesthetics and themes of the canzone, appropriateness of stylistic regis-ters, and so forth.

Earlier in his life, at the time he wrote the *Vita Nuova*, which Emerson deeply appreciated, Dante had defined poetry in strictly subjective terms. The *Vita Nuova* essentially tells the story of Dante's youthful love for Beatrice as both a sentimental education and a poetic apprenticeship. And because then he had understood the law of his love as exclusive of all objective reality (politics, the social realities of the city of Florence, the facts that would define the beloved), he had also understood poetry as the secret code of a secret passion, as the pursuit of the mysterious signs of Beatrice's luminous apparition in the middle of an unreal and unnamed city. Caught in the ghostly world of his own mind, besieged by memories and fears, overwhelmed by the death of Beatrice, Dante turns poetry into the solitary language of the hieroglyphs of love's compulsions.

But in the *De Vulgari Eloquentia* poetry is invested with a new status. "Poetry," Dante says in an astonishing formula, "is a rhetorical art set to music." The definition conveys primarily the notion of the poet's neces-sary observance of rhetorical rules to be coupled with the versifier's musical gift. The essence of poetry, then, lies in communicating the melody of thought, and this melody can only be the result of the tension between the discipline of rhetorical precision and the elusive resonance of rhythm. But because rhetoric and music, which are said to make up poetry, are two of the seven liberal arts, the definition projects poetry as an activity that encompasses disparate and discordant realms of experience, is irreducible to any one of them, and cuts across and binds them together.

In his essay on Dante's theories of language, Longfellow does not belabor the implications of this definition of poetry. He does not fail, however, to rightly insist that in the *De Vulgari Eloquentia* Dante views poetry as part of the larger reality of language (legal, political, and so on) he seeks to forge. We are told that Dante theorizes what eventually the *Divine Comedy* will deliver: a national idiom made of scraps drawn from the various dialects that divide the Italian language. Such a language exists already everywhere in parts, "but nowhere as a whole, save in the pages of the classic writer."[1] Longfellow's conception of the poet who imaginatively brings to life a language nourished by the soil of every province closely echoes the insights of eighteenth-century philosophers of language, such as Cesarotti. But it recalls, above all, the thought of a kindred soul of Emerson's, the philosopher Giambattista Vico, who believes in the power of the poetic imagination to bind together and sustain the various and discordant discourses of the tribe. As Emerson was later to intuit, Vico understands Dante, whom he calls the Tuscan Homer, as the poet-encyclopedist who in the *Divine Comedy* gives a representation of the many voices, cadences, styles, and, in one word, dialects of Italy.

In more recent times American poets' study of Dante has never really cast aside Emerson's oracular image of Dante's majestic intellect, of the poet whose dreams feed invariably upon infinity. This image, however, becomes the somewhat muted metaphysical underpinning for a sober assessment of Dante the craftsman, of the concrete ways in which he

---

1. Henry Wadsworth Longfellow, "A History of the Italian Language and Dialects (1832)," in *Dante in America: The First Two Centuries*, ed. A. Bartlett Giamatti (Binghamton, N.Y.: Medieval and Renaissance Texts and Studies, 1983), 42.

gives body to the soul of the language. For poets such as Pound, Eliot, and Tate, to mention those who explicitly recognize Dante's impact on their poetry, Dante's style, which they occasionally discuss in detail, is both the basis and sign of his metaphysical system: it is the vehicle by which his metaphysics becomes a personal experience, a daily labor that penetrates and shapes his imagination.

In a justly famous essay, "The Symbolic Imagination: The Mirrors of Dante," Allen Tate examines the configuration of themes and images (light, visibility, words) in Dante's poem as the key to his poetics of analogy, to the prodigious resemblances Dante's imagination posits between divergent realms of the human and the divine, the natural and the supernatural. Ezra Pound, on the other hand, who understood the virtue of stylistic discipline ("the mastery of any art," he once wrote, "is the work of a lifetime"), was drawn more than any other poet to what one can call the earthiness of Dante's craft. In reviewing Laurence Binyon's English translation of the *Inferno*, Pound cites the celebrated maxim by Spinoza: "The love of a thing consists in the understanding of its perfection."[2] Consistently with the maxim, he proceeds to dismantle the mechanism of Binyon's rendition and scrupulously turns his attention to Binyon's avoidance of pseudomagniloquence "of puffed words," which is generally alien to Dante's habit of thought; he praises his penchant for monosyllables and for aiming to capture the "sharp, clear quality of the original *sound* as a whole" by not imitating Dante's feminine rhymes; he damns him for a number of minutiae ("freckled" for "gaetta" in *Inferno* I appears to him as "not very good." But I suspect he would have liked Heaney's literal and direct "spotted"). T. S. Eliot, in a talk delivered at the Italian Institute in London in 1951 and later published as "What Dante Means to Me," probes the difficulties he experienced in seeking to approximate Dante's terza rima in English. He reminds us that *The Triumph of Life*, Shelley's last and greatest poem, deploys the terza rima at the great risk of failing (the poem was left unfinished). He ends by suggesting the adoption of an alternation of

2. Ezra Pound, "Hell. A Review of Dante's *Inferno* translated into English Triple Rhyme, by Laurence Binyon," in *Dante in America: The First Two Centuries*, ed. A. B. Giamatti, 175–86.

"unrhymed masculine and feminine terminations, as the nearest way of giving the light effect of the rhyme in Italian."[3]

These poets' attention to the details and technical construction of Dante's verse is certainly determined by the challenge of translating the *Divine Comedy* into English. But, in effect, their care for the poet's craft leads them to the inner quality and design of Dante's fabric, to the core of the project he pursues as an immense but not impossible task of writing. It is a commonplace to say that it is impossible to translate poetry. Dante himself buttresses this view as he writes in a passage from his *Convivio* that "no discourse harmonized with the Muses' bonds can be translated from its own dialect into another without the destruction of all its sweetness and harmony."[4]

No doubt the resonances achieved through alliterative effects, through repeated rhymes and distribution of consonants and vowels, and sundry other techniques constitute what is known as the poetic effect, which, though lost in translation, can be regained via the translators' imaginative re-creation of the original. Yet, we have all become aware in the wake of Walter Benjamin's essay on translation that any original Ur-text is itself always a displaced version of an ideal form and that the original text inevitably falls short of the poet's absolute intuition. As a matter of fact, Dante himself, who never stops thinking about language both as a medium and as a way of being, understands translation as the very metaphor of poetry at the moment in which he perceives as unavoidable the discrepancy between his words and his vision. An instance of such an insight occurs at the opening of Canto XXXII of the *Inferno*. As the pilgrim approaches the bottom of the universe, the poet says in Digges's rendition:

> Were there a language dark enough to speak
> truly of that hole harrowed by crags
> gravity itself could not fall through to,

3. T. S. Eliot, "A Talk on Dante," in *Dante in America*, 219–227.
4. The passage is found in Dante's *Convivio* (*Banquet*) I, xvii, 13–15. The translation is taken from *Literary Criticism of Dante Alighieri;* trans. and ed. by Robert S. Haller (Lincoln and London: University of Nebraska Press, 1973), 72.

I could taste the salt of my conception.
    But words are abstract, sadly approximate,
      dull with use. I'm afraid to move my mouth,
Afraid to shape sounds which might conjure
    the bottom of the universe, mouth which once
      knew no more than the sweet suck of *mama*,
Papa. May the voices the stones followed down
    the mountain all the way to Thebes find me
      as they found Amphion's lyre, here bear witness.

Digges gives here a free rendition of Dante's text, yet she fully captures the sound of Dante's shuttle between the familiar and the eerie, as well as his sense of the inadequacy of the child's halting talk to represent the infinite horrors of this topsy-turvy world, which only the epic voice of the mythic Amphion can approximate. More than that, the passage dramatizes Dante's selection of a style—the modulations of a dark language or of a hard, stony style commensurate to the intractable, tragic matter of treachery he is about to witness.

    This concern with a discrete style of representation is not unusual in the unfolding of the *Divine Comedy*. In this case the discrete style Dante evokes is that of the stony rhymes he had written earlier in his life. One could extend the present recollection of the "stony style" into nothing less than a general principle of Dante's poetic composition. As Vico, Emerson, and Longfellow have seen in their different ways, the poem is an encyclopedia of languages or dialects: Dante adopts a variety of styles because style for him is a mode of vision, a viewpoint on the world and oneself. This principle in turn suggests that because the poem has such an appearance of solid unity, one can easily forget that it is made up of so many different languages and scraps of traditions.

    These various languages are all found in the poem, for Dante is not the man to ever dismiss the hard-won experiences he has accumulated over the years of his life. From this essential perspective the *Divine Comedy* records the poet's encounters with the languages of the rhetorical and classical traditions, of the natural sciences, of the songs of the wandering Provençal minstrels and the French trouvères, of the religious-prophetic schools, and the like. All together these strands manage to communicate the many-sidedness and the restlessness of Dante's spirit. What exactly are these strands, and how do they figure in the poem? For the sake of clarity I will isolate only a few of them.

Dante's early education was marked by the study of the Latin poets (Virgil, Ovid, Lucan, and so on). But he also read the then popular works of French literature (the Charlemagne epics and the Arthurian romances, such as *Tristan* and *Lancelot of the Lake*). In the *De Vulgari Eloquentia* he will refer to these romances as *ambages pulcherrimae*—most beautiful labyrinths or intricate mazes of the imagination that inform the narrative and novelistic movement of Canto V of the *Inferno*.

But the strongest lyrical influence on Dante came from Provence. The songs of Peire Vidal, Bertran de Born, Arnaut Daniel (whom Dante in *Purgatorio* will hail as the "welder of the mother tongue"), and Peire d'Auvergne shape the structure and lexicon of his love-lyrics. From Peire d'Auvergne, who writes exquisite winter love songs, Dante learns the harsh sounds (with the rhymes in *-orca, -arco, -etra, -armo*, and so forth) he deploys in the "stony rhymes" and in the lower cantos of the *Inferno*. It is even likely, as has so often been suggested, that Dante's terza rima is a brilliantly simplified version of Arnaut's sestina. At any rate, the mingling of narrative and lyric in the *Vita Nuova* certainly recalls the *razos* of the Provençal poets.

What proved decisive, however, in the writing of the *Vita Nuova*, in the course of which Dante reelaborates the Sweet New Style, is his friendship with Guido Cavalcanti, "the first of my friends," to whom he addresses the work. As a thinker, Guido, who was older than Dante, was rumored to have Averroistic leanings, which means that he was interested in natural philosophy and did not believe in the immortality of the soul. As a poet, Guido has grasped the essence of the New Style, the originator of which was Guido Guinizelli. Cavalcanti, like Guinizelli, couches the Provençal traditions of love poetry in a philosophical, scholastic language, which to Dante, however, seemed too abstract, highblown, and cerebral. If in the *Vita Nuova* Dante adheres in part to these theories of poetry and thinks of poetry as a pure experience of the mind of love (to be associated at most with the music of Casella and the paintings of Giotto), he will later move away from them in the conviction that poetry is the force shaping all the private and public discourses of man.

The depth of Cavalcanti's friendship for Dante can be gauged by the sonnet he sends to Dante when, after the death of Beatrice (1290), Dante seemed to waste his talent and his life by associating himself with dissolute, goliardic figures (Cecco Angiolieri, Forese Donati, and others) the aristocratic and haughty Cavalcanti simply found too vulgar. Eventually, Dante was to learn that, however repellent the moral values of these poets were, he had benefited immensely from associating with them. Cecco's comic poems about a faithless, sensual woman, Becchina, who is everything Beatrice cannot be; his sonnets to Dante in which Cecco drags him down to his own world ("Dante, if I breakfast at other men's tables, you dine at them; if I bite into the fat, you nibble at bacon . . ."); and his invectives against the stinginess of his father, to mention a few of his themes, turn into wares for Dante's own *Commedia* as well as for "comedy of devils" in *Inferno* XIX and XXII.

The above are only some of the styles or languages Dante makes available in the *Inferno*. Each canto, in effect, has its own specificity of style, from the "blurred shadows" of Canto I (as Ungaretti in a memorable essay refers to the lyrical substance of this canto) to the prophetic language punctuating the canto of the ecclesiastic simony (*Inferno* XIX); from the apocalyptic recasting of Nebuchadnezzar's dream (Daniel 2:31 ff.) in *Inferno* XIV to the didactic language of *Inferno* XV where Dante meets his teacher, Brunetto Latini; from the tragedy of Pier delle Vigne in Canto XIII to that of Bertran de Born in XXVIII, to that of Ulysses in Canto XXVI (which comes forth as the tragedy of Hellenism), to that of Ugolino in *Inferno* XXXIII.

The present translations of the cantos of the *Inferno*, in their different cadences and rhythms, convey the wide array of tonalities with which Dante's style reverberates and through which he establishes a transversal unity to the multiple plots and the heterogeneous experiences of his imaginary world. This collective enterprise, whereby different voices of today's American poetry turn Dante into English, is an extraordinary venture that responds most creatively to the essence of the disparate rhythms in Dante's voice: a vast chamber of resonance in which discordant strains—the bedlam of taverns, the lovers' whispers in enclosed gardens, the careful pitch of courtiers, the wild screams of battlefields, the noises of the streets—vibrate and still touch us. His polyglot voice, which Emerson dreamt for the yet-to-come grand poem of America, now echoes in the rich personal modulations of the translation of the present volume.

—Giuseppe Mazzotta
Yale University

NOTES

Most of the notes that follow have been compiled with the help of the work by Charles S. Singleton, John D. Sinclair, Allen Mandelbaum, Dorothy Sayers, C. H. Grandgent (in the Laurence Binyon translation), Henry Wadsworth Longfellow, Mark Musa, and the Carlyle-Okey-Wicksteed group, scholars and translators all. To them, the translators of this volume are indebted. —D.H.

CANTO I / *Seamus Heaney*

The Divine Comedy is a poem about turning toward the light, and the first canto rehearses in miniature the overall drama of the protagonist's struggle toward illumination. The poem is, however, more an allegory than an autobiography, so the opening lines speak about "the journey of *our* life," and the animals that assail Dante on the way up the mountain represent perils that the soul typically faces as it attempts to escape from the dark wood of a sinful state. The sunlit mountain, embodying a promise of release and salvation, is therefore an aspect of Mount Purgatory, which Dante will ascend in the second *cantiche* of the poem; and through Purgatory he will finally arrive at the total illumination of his vision in Paradise.

In the course of the poem, Dante's progress toward greater spiritual vision is assisted by two guides, the poet Virgil and Dante's own beloved Beatrice—a girl whom he had loved in Florence and who manifested to him (in life and after her early death) the glory of heaven itself. Beatrice therefore becomes an image of all that the soul can attain to by the action of Divine Grace as it is mediated through the Church, the Sacraments, and the intercession of the Blessed Virgin with her son, Jesus Christ. Virgil, on the other hand, represents the best that mankind can attain without the aid of Christian Revelation. He is the image of Human Wisdom, and represents the highest functioning of poetry, philosophy, and morality as they strive toward the attainment of natural perfection and prepare the soul for the operation of Divine Grace.

Virgil also appears in the poem as a vital link between the world of Imperial Rome and the world of the Holy Roman Empire. His status in medieval Christianity was that of a prophet suspended between the dispensations of the Old Testament and the New Testament, although to this general apprehension of his central place in the cultural and religious traditions of Europe, Dante brings the additional intensity and gratitude of a poet paying homage to a great predecessor.

16 The moment of turning toward the light, of "conversion," reinforced by the associations of the sun with Christ in His glory.

31–54 The leopard, the lion, and the she-wolf have been identified by Dorothy Sayers as images of Lust, Pride, and Avarice, the sins of Youth, Manhood, and Age; perhaps they can be thought of also as aspects of self-indulgence, violence, and malicious fraudulence or greed. The greed of the she-wolf has sometimes been taken as an indirect condemnation of a corrupt and worldly Church.

60 Dante is pushed back toward the dark wood: metaphorically, he comes to a place where light cannot be uttered by the sun.

63 This line repeats the mingling of aural and visual figures that has just occurred at line 60. Dante cannot "make out" Virgil clearly, perhaps because a ghost cannot speak until it is addressed; perhaps because of his own dulled capacities as one entrapped in the ways of sin; or it may be that an allusion is intended to the way in which the literature and learning of the classical past have fallen into neglect.

69–75 The Latin poet Virgil (Publius Virgilius Maro, 70 B.C.–19 B.C.) published pastoral and didactic poems, but in Dante's imagination his great exemplary force derives from his epic, the *Aeneid*. It tells of the founding of Rome by Aeneas, a survivor of the destruction of Troy, and in the course of that narrative it also recounts the story of Aeneas' journey to meet his father's shade in the underworld. Thus, the *Aeneid* prefigures the tale of Dante's own underground journey in *The Inferno*, as well as giving an account of the foundation of a civilization that would eventually develop into the Roman Catholicism of medieval times.

100 *The Hound:* An image of some hoped-for savior, a political figure who will establish a spiritually cleansed world empire. The apocalyptic force of The Hound is increased by his being an emanation of attributes associated with the Godhead—wisdom, love, and power.

104 This line has been much discussed and is subject to two main interpretations. I have (without compelling reasons) gone for the reading that takes "Feltro" as a place name, and situates the hound's birthplace between (say) Feltre in Venetia and Montifeltro in Romagna. But equally attractive is the reading that translates "feltro" as felt, or frieze cloth, and understands the line to predict a "savior" coming from those who wear this humble cloth and do not "glut . . . on ground or riches."

107 In the *Aeneid*, Camilla, Turnus, Nisus, and Euryalus all died in the war waged against the native Italians by Aeneas, the original precursor of the Roman *imperium*.

122–25 Virgil, who lived before the coming of Christ and was thus deprived of the graces of Christ's Redemption, is confined to Limbo; he therefore must leave Dante once he comes to the threshold of heaven, where Beatrice—"a soul worthier than I"—will take charge of his farther ascent.

133 *St. Peter's Gate:* the entry into Purgatory.

CANTO II / *Seamus Heaney*

In the classical epic, many of the struggles and projects of the heroes and heroines are initiated in the world of the gods. This supernatural dimension of epic narrative is paralleled here by Virgil's revelation of the concern displayed by Beatrice, Lucy, and the Virgin Mary herself in the court of heaven over Dante's fate. Dante's personal struggle to get free of the dark wood is thus set in a cosmic framework and the meaning of each element in his story gets amplified within a celestial acoustic. In the opening exchanges, however, it is the literary and historical foreshadowings of the otherworldly journey that preoccupy the poet, as he puts his own account of the crossing to eternity in the context of journeys taken by Aeneas and St. Paul.

7 The invocation of the muses is an epic convention that Dante deliberately repeats. Note also that the journey is presented not as a dream vision but as a remembered event.

13 *The father of Silvius:* Aeneas, whose journey to the underworld is narrated by Virgil in Book VI of the *Aeneid*.

17 *The Adversary of all things evil:* God.

28 *The Chosen Vessel:* St. Paul, who in 2 Corinthians XII speaks of a "man in Christ"—himself—"caught up as far as the third heaven," and who there "heard words too sacred to tell." There was also a fourth-century apocryphal book of *The Apocalypse of St. Paul*.

52 Virgil was in Limbo, "in suspense" between the pains of hell and the bliss of salvation, when he was called by Beatrice. The story of Dante's love for Beatrice is told in his early poem sequence, *La Vita Nuova*. In *The Divine Comedy* she appears as a divinely suffused presence, a sign of the more abundant life to which revealed religion gives access.

83–84 Beatrice has come out of heaven to Virgil at some spot in the infernal regions under the earth, and since earth itself is at the center of this universe, the spot where they meet is at "the deep center"—farthest away from "the spacious zone" of the outermost sphere, the sphere of empyrean heaven. Beatrice is therefore here literally out of her element, but has been made immune, physically and psychologically, to the sufferings that surround her when she leaves heaven.

94–114 The sequence of events is as follows: The Blessed Virgin—"a gentle lady"—speaks to Lucy—probably the third-century virgin martyr who was known as the patron of weak eyesight and thus associated with the retrieval of true vision. She asks Lucy to take heed of Dante's plight. Lucy then brings explicit instructions to Beatrice—who is sitting with Rachel, a figure representative of the contemplative life—and Beatrice tells how she proceeded to fulfill these instructions by turning to Virgil for his assistance.

CANTO III / *Seamus Heaney*

The world that Dante invents in *The Divine Comedy* is made up of elements drawn from the classical pagan world and from the doctrines and history of Christianity as they had been elaborated in his own time. Thus his picture of hell is taken partly from Virgil's *Aeneid*, where Charon "poles the boat, tends the sails, and in his murky craft conveys the dead." But it is partly also a scholastic *paysage moralisé* in which the different gradations of spiritual failure (ranging from satanic malignity to lukewarm goodness) find themselves expressed by a typical geography and a representative cast of characters. Thus the souls of those who lived in a vague and uncommitted tolerance—what Dorothy Sayers called "a cautious cowardice for which no decision is ever final"—are not placed in hell proper but in the ante-hell described in this canto, where they rush about uselessly in constantly changing directions.

37 The morally neutral are placed with the angels who did not join with Satan in his rebellion against God and yet did not join forces with God's angels, either.

52–57 An example of the symmetry of the punishment that Dante devises in hell for those who sinned on earth: Those who failed to pursue a definite direction and follow one banner during their lifetime spend all eternity in futile pursuit of a banner that keeps going in *all* directions.

59–60 *The shade of him | Who made the great refusal:* Pope Celestine V. He was elected pope in 1294 at the age of eighty, but abdicated five months later. This refusal of responsibility ushered in the papacy of Boniface VIII, whom Dante regarded as a deplorable holder of the office.

71 *Acheron:* the first of the great rivers of hell, part of the infernal geography that Dante borrowed from the classics.

83 *an old man:* Charon, the ferryman of the dead.

88–89 Charon recognizes that Dante is alive, but he also has knowledge that the poet is not destined to go to hell after his death.

95–96 Virgil reveals that God in heaven has permitted this suspension of the usual laws of entry into hell.

CANTO IV | *Mark Strand*

1–3 Borne across the river Acheron in his sleep, Dante awakens at the edge of an abyss, and enters the first circle of the Inferno, the Limbo of the Unbaptized.

53 *a mighty lord:* refers to Christ, who is never mentioned by name in the Inferno. Virgil died in 19 B.C., and thus arrived in Limbo fifty-three years before Christ descended there to rescue the souls of the patriarchs ("The Harrowing of Hell").

55 *our first father's shade:* refers to Adam.

85 The sword symbolizes Homer's epic of the Trojan War.

107 *a noble castle:* the Palace of Wisdom. Its seven surrounding walls represent the four moral virtues (prudence, temperance, fortitude, and justice) and the three intellectual virtues (understanding, knowledge, and wisdom).

108–09 Longfellow notes that "the fair rivulet" ("the lovely moat") is Eloquence, which Dante does not seem to consider a very profound matter, as he and Virgil pass over it as if it were dry ground ("solid ground").

110 The gates symbolize the seven liberal arts of the trivium (grammar, logic, and rhetoric) and the quadrivium (music, arithmetic, geometry, and astronomy) which afford access to knowledge.

121 *Electra:* daughter of Atlas, and mother of Dardanus, who founded Troy.

124 *Camilla:* a maiden warrior; *Penthesilea:* queen of the Amazons.

126–28 *Lavinia:* the wife of Aeneas; *Brutus:* a foe of the Tarquins; *Lucretia:* wife of Collatinus; *Julia:* daughter of Caesar, wife of Pompey; *Marcia:* wife of Cato of Utica; *Cornelia:* daughter of Scipio Africanus, mother of the Gracchi.

129 *Saladin:* the model of chivalry. He was sultan of Egypt and Syria in the twelfth century, and was defeated several times by Richard the Lion-Heart.

131 *the master of those who know:* Aristotle.

141 *Tully:* Cicero, the great Roman orator, philosopher, and statesman; *Linus:* a mythical Greek poet.

143 *Hippocrates, Galen, and Avicenna:* three famous physicians of Greece, Mysia, and Turkestan.

144 *Averroës:* a twelfth-century Spanish Moorish scholar and philosopher whose "Commentary" was on the works of Aristotle.

148 *the company of six shrinks to only two:* the two are Virgil and Dante.

CANTO V / *Daniel Halpern*

1–2 Hell narrows as it goes deeper; the circles grow smaller, like a funnel.

4 *Minos:* judge of the dead. He is a monster taken from classical mythology. The offspring of Europa and Zeus, and once King of Crete, he was known for his fairness and wisdom.

58–59 *Semiramis:* Queen of Assyria, she succeeded her husband, Ninus, who founded Nineveh, and was known as much for her interest in the pleasures of the body as in ruling her people. She is credited with having legalized incest.

61 This is Dido, Queen of Carthage, whose story is told by Virgil in the *Aeneid*—a tale of doomed love for Aeneas, the Trojan leader, and her infidelity to Sichaeus, her dead husband, to whom she swore everlasting faithfulness. She commits suicide when Aeneas, reminded by the gods of his ultimate destiny, leaves for Italy to found Rome.

63 *Cleopatra:* daughter of the last King of Egypt; became Queen of Egypt with the help of Julius Caesar. She then lived with Mark Antony until his death. She later killed herself with a poisonous asp.

64 *Helen:* the wife of Menelaus, King of Sparta. Her abduction by Paris caused the Trojan War.

65 Medieval accounts, which differ from Homer's, have Paris killing Achilles in the temple of Apollo, where the latter went with the intention of marrying the beautiful Trojan Polyxena, sister of Paris and daughter of Hecuba and Priam.

67 *Paris:* son of Priam, King of Troy; he is credited with starting the Trojan War by kidnapping Helen. Tristan, the lover of Yseult in the famous medieval French romance, was killed by her husband—also Tristan's uncle.

74 Paolo and Francesca of Rimini. Francesca married Paolo's brother Gianciotto, but fell in love with Paolo. When Gianciotto discovered this, he killed them both.

97 The town is Ravenna, located near the Adriatic coast, at the mouth of the Po River.

107 *Caina:* "Cain's hell," located in the ninth and deepest circle of Hell (Cocytus), that region reserved for those who sinned against their family—as in Cain killing Abel. Caina awaits Gianciotto, who in 1300 was still alive.

123 The teacher referred to here is Virgil.

127 They were reading a book about Lancelot, the most famous knight of King Arthur's Round Table, who fell in love with Guinevere, King Arthur's wife.

137 *Gallehault:* a character in the book they were reading who acted as a go-between for Lancelot and Guinevere—so for Dante's purposes, the author who created the tale and the book itself serve as a kind of intermediary for Paolo and Francesca.

CANTO VI / *Galway Kinnell*

58 *Ciacco:* a nickname meaning "hog."

64ff. Having the power of a soul in hell to know past and future events, Ciacco tells Dante of the happenings in Florence in the years immediately after 1300, the fictitious date of the poem.

69 *one:* Pope Boniface VIII.

73 *two:* It is often thought that Dante meant one of them to be himself.

79–81 For Farinata, see below, Canto X, 32; for Tegghiaio and Rusticucci, Canto XVI, 36–38; and for Mosca, Canto XXVIII, 96. Arrigo is not mentioned again.

96 *the adverse power:* Christ.

106 *philosophy:* The doctrines of Aristotle come down through Aquinas.

115 *Plutus:* Plutus, god of riches, was not always distinguished from Pluto, god of the underworld.

CANTO VII / *Cynthia Macdonald*

1 *Pape Satan aleppe:* This is a cryptic phrase. It seems to be addressed to Satan. *Pape* may be a form of "portmanteau" invention, because it combines or refers to words the reader does know. For example, *Pape* might relate to *papà* (father), to *Pàpa* (Pope), to *pàpera* (goose, or error in pronunciation), or to *papesco* (popish). This portmanteau reading of *Pape* would certainly attach negative connotations to the figure of the pope, a reading that fits with Dante's antagonism toward Pope Boniface VII (1294–1303). Beatrice's last words to Dante in the *Paradiso* are a violent condemnation of Boniface (*Paradiso*, XXX, 148).

Some early scholars took *Pape* to be related to the Latin word *papae*, an interjection that "expresses the state of mind called astonishment and marvel" (*Ottimo Commento*). *Aleppe* is usually identified with the first letter of the Hebrew alphabet, *aleph*, which is used as an expression of grief.

2 Plutus is the god of wealth; Pluto, the god of the underworld. In classical times, and still in fourteenth-century Florence, they were connected, often seen as one and the same.

18 In the Italian, *'l mal de l'universe tutto insacca. Insacca* is often translated as "ensacked" or "insacked." I've chosen "banked," with its connotations both of place and of hoarding and spending, and brought the "sack" in only in the next tercet.

22 The famous whirlpool in the Straits of Messina is considered particularly dangerous because it is partnered with the rock Scylla. Virgil described it this way in the *Aeneid* (III, 420–23): Scylla stands guard on the left side; Charybdis lies in wait on the left, where, in the depth of her wildness, she sucks vast waves into her pit, then regurgitates them, dashing them against the stars.

23 In the Italian, *ridda:* a round dance. Once again, this introduces the theme of the circle. The circles of Hell through which Dante and Virgil are traveling are inlaid with many other kinds of circles. In the next twelve tercets the hoarders and spenders are antagonists who collide over and over, only to reverse and collide again. Each collision results in another circle, formed appropriately from inharmonious, clashing elements. The narrative slows down in these tercets, not

because the concepts are particularly complicated, but perhaps because Dante wanted to keep the reader trapped in the entrapping dance.

27 In the Italian, *pesl:* weights composed of the wealth the hoarders and spenders loved too well.

36 Dante's heart may have felt punctured because the hoarders and spenders were peculiarly close to him. Dante's father was probably a lender and money changer who, as a result of his profession, accumulated large land holdings in the area of Florence.

61–72 There are an unusually large number of hard *c* (k) sounds throughout these tercets, particularly in the end words *anche, tocche, branche, sciocche,* and *'mbocche,* as if a message is being pounded home, or, perhaps more accurately, given the meaning of *'mbocche,* "take into the mouth," or "swallow," as if Dante is being force-fed.

72–96 In these tercets Dante discourses on Fortune. The presentation gives an unclear or ambivalent picture. Fortune retains her classical role as the female figure within a wheel (the wheel of Fortune, another circle) who rules men's fortunes, but with the introduction of "the Wisest One" and what I've translated as "the angel/sage" we know from the *Convivio* and other parts of the *Divine Comedy* that Dante is introducing the intelligences and their leader. Dante says in the *Convivio* that in Plato's time, intelligences were gods and goddesses. But in these tercets he uses the word to mean angels. Translators have tried ministers, intelligences, guides, a general ministress, a universal ruler, etc. The angels and their leader are clearly post-Virgil Christian figures. The dictatorial pre-Christian Fortune and the later, more benevolent angels are somewhat antithetical to each other, almost another form of the counterdance.

103 In the Italian, *L'acqua:* the river Acheron which completely circles Hell, then runs under the first four circles and emerges here as the river Styx and the marsh it creates.

CANTO VIII / *Cynthia Macdonald*

1–2 A lot has been written about the way the narrative loops back in these lines. Dante begins Canto VIII by saying he will continue the narrative, but then goes back to describe the approach to the tower, which had already been reached in the last line of VII. Charles Singleton calls it "extraordinary" and says that Boccaccio and the *Anonimo fiorentino* believed that Dante wrote the first seven cantos before his exile, left them behind in Florence, and later, when they were sent to him, mirrored his own interruption by interrupting the forward progress of the narrative.

4 Boccaccio says that it was the custom to send news of war by setting one signal fire or two, which could be seen by surrounding towns and villages.

13–15 Another moment of opposition (like the "Fortune" passage in Canto VII). First we see the boat as if it were an arrow speeding away from the archer's bow, but at the end of the canto the boat is speeding toward Dante and Virgil. Perhaps the turn at the end of the metaphor gives a mixed message about who the target is.

19 *Phlegyas:* the son of Mars, who set fire to Apollo's temple because Apollo had raped his daughter. Apollo punished him by sending him to the place in the lower world

reserved for those who sinned against the gods. Dante makes Phlegyas the boatman of the Styx. He, full of wrath, guards the Fifth Circle, where the wrathful are.

18–20 Phlegyas believes he's captured another soul, but Virgil lets him know he hasn't "got" Dante (because Dante is alive).

36–63 *Filippo Argenti:* a Florentine knight known for his dreadful temper, who so flaunted his fortune that he had his horse shod with silver; thus the name Argenti. He was a member of the Adimari family, which opposed Dante and fought to maintain his banishment from Florence. Thus, the bitterness Dante displays toward him in this passage is understandable. He expresses his wish to see Argenti submerged in the thick stew (literally *broda,* "broth") of the bog. What is surprising is that Virgil not only tells him that his wish will be fulfilled, he praises Dante: "Indignant soul, blest is the one who bore you in her womb" (lines 44–45), and he says nothing when Dante thanks God as he watches the angry horde rend Argenti. This permitted, even blessed, enactment of wrath in the circle of the wrathful is strange.

62 In the Italian, *bizzaro:* people who are quickly angered and refuse to be mollified. Singleton says this word is uniquely Florentine; so I have translated it as "with Florentine discord."

68 It is interesting to note that the city called Dite in Italian has always been translated into English as Dis, the name the Romans gave Pluto. But they called his city Ditis, which is closer to Dite.

69 *its vast battalions:* Satan's army of demons.

70 *mosques:* indicates that Dis is a city of infidels.

109 Here Dante uses the present tense in a peculiar way, not as he did earlier in the canto (lines 58–60), but in a way that occurs occasionally throughout the *Inferno.* Perhaps tense shifts of this type occur in moments of extreme tension. Certainly this passage is one of those moments.

111 *"yes" and "no":* indicates both uncertainty about the outcome of Virgil's negotiation and Dante's ability to return to the world.

124–26 Although Christ is not mentioned in the Italian, these lines refer to His breaking down the outer gate of Hell when He arrived there from Limbo. Satan and the demons tried to stop His passage, but He shattered the lock and that gate was never locked again.

128 *those dead words:* the words over the gate to Hell which begin Canto III. I've chosen to quote a brief fragment of them here.

129 Virgil knows that the divine messenger who will open the gates of Dis has almost reached them.

CANTO IX / *Amy Clampitt*

24–28 The notion, widely held among medieval Christians, that witches had power over both the living and the dead is implicit in the reference to the sorceress Erichtho and Virgil's earlier errand into the deepest circle of hell.

31 *This marsh:* The river Styx is described as a marshy one in the sixth book of the *Aeneid.* Virgil's references derive in turn from the *Iliad,* whose eighth book contains several mentions of it.

32 *The doleful metropolis:* the city of Dis, the stronghold of Satan and his rebel angels.

37–51 The Furies (their Greek name, the Erinyes, means "angry ones") in the *Aeneid* have an almost proprietary association with the river Styx. The "household" they serve (line 43) is that of Proserpina, the bride of Pluto and queen of the underworld.

52 Medusa, one of the Gorgons, is to be found in the underworld of Homer as well as of Virgil. According to pagan mythology, she was so frightful that whoever looked at her was turned to stone.

54 Once again, the sixth book of the *Aeneid* is Dante's source for the reference to Theseus, who made a visit to the realm of Tartarus in an effort to carry Proserpina back to the world above.

80 The one "moving dry of foot across the Styx" is the help promised by Beatrice in Canto II.

98 Like Theseus, Hercules made a heroic foray into Tartarus, from which he tried to drag the infernal watchdog Cerberus by a chain about the neck. Again, the sixth book of the *Aeneid* is Dante's source, as the eighth book of the *Iliad* is Virgil's.

112–14 Arles, in Provence, and Pola, in Istria, are the sites of ancient burial places.

CANTO X / *Amy Clampitt*

10–12 The reference is to the book of the biblical prophet Joel, 3:12: "Let the heathen be wakened, and come up to the valley of Jehoshaphat, for there will I sit to judge all the heathen round about me."

22 The speaker is Manente degli Uberti, known as Farinata, a leader of the party of the Ghibellines, whose name has already been mentioned in Canto VI, line 79. He died in 1264, a year before Dante was born. A few years later the Inquisition posthumously declared him and his family guilty of heresy; his bones were exhumed and his property confiscated.

40–51 The conversation has to do with the political feuds of the time. Dante, whose family belonged to the petty nobility (so that Farinata has evident difficulty in placing them), was allied with the Guelphs, against whom Farinata had been victorious in 1248 and again in 1260. But the Guelphs later returned to Florence and expelled the Ghibellines.

52–60 The second speaker is Cavalcante de' Cavalcanti, father of Dante's close friend, the poet Guido Cavalcanti.

63 The identity of the one "whom . . . your Guido scoffed at" is not entirely clear, but is presumably Virgil.

73–75 The conversation here has to do with the failure of the Ghibellines to reestablish themselves in Florence.

79 *That queen* is Hecate, the infernal goddess of the moon, who is invoked by witches.

82 Farinata, able to discern the shape of future events (though deprived of any clear certainty about what is occurring at a given moment), predicts the decree of exile against Dante that is to occur in 1302, two years after the events of the poem, and the troubles to come.

82–90 At the battle of Montaperti in 1260, the Guelphs were crushingly defeated by a combined force of Germans, Sienese, and Ghibelline exiles from Florence. It was following this "bloody rout" that Farinata prevailed in his counsel against the proposed sack of Florence.

119–20 The emperor Frederick II (1212–1250) was regarded as a materialist and is thus associated with the Epicureans. Cardinal Ottaviano degli Ubaldini, who came of a Ghibelline family and was an opponent of Frederick, is reported to have said, "If there is a soul, I have lost mine a thousand times for the Ghibellines."

130–31 These lines refer to Beatrice.

C A N T O   X I / *Jorie Graham*

A note on form: Although I have retained, in essence, the motion of Dante's stanzas, I have also given myself permission to spring their formal organization open from time to time. Underneath the stanzas there is, of course, the rhythm of two men walking and talking and thinking and seeing. The Italian has always seemed to me full of interruptions, misapprehensions, misapprehensions—some fear, some awe of course—but also some disagreement. I used the stanzas, and the silences they afforded me, to try to enact that drama, as well as the drama of the composing poet's distance—the strain of recovery, memory, vision.

8–9 Singleton notes that Emperor Anastasius—who ruled from 491 to 518—not Pope Anastasius, his contemporary, is said to have been led by Photinus, a deacon of Thessalonia, into the heresy of Acacius (Patriarch of Constantinople). Acacius denied the divine origin of Christ, holding that He was naturally begotten and conceived.

58 Usurers were also known as Caorsines, after the French town of Caorse, where they were numerous.

87 This is a specific reference to a distinction drawn by Aristotle in the Nicomachean Ethics (VII, 1, 1145): "Now, making a new start, we must indicate that there are three kinds of dispositions in moral practice to be avoided: vice, incontinence, and brutishness."

102 Again, Singleton notes the reference here is to Aristotle's *Metaphysics* and, two verses farther down, to his *Physics*.

109–11 These verses echo Genesis 3:17, 19, "In toil shall you eat of it all the days of your life. . . . In the sweat of your brow you shall eat bread." Also II Thess. 3:10, "If any man work not, neither let him eat." Also, finally, God's command to Eve in Genesis 1:28, "Be fruitful and multiply . . . replenish the earth and subdue it . . ."

119 Dante is actually referring to the constellation of the Fishes, or Pisces. As it is the time of the vernal equinox and the sun is in Aries, Pisces is the zodiacal sign immediately preceding the sun and begins to rise about four A.M. The canto ends, therefore, at the break of day on Holy Saturday. "Cauris" is the Romans' northwest wind.

C A N T O   X I I / *Jorie Graham*

4–10 Dante is comparing this massive scree to the Stavini di Marco, a vast fall of rocks due to a landslide twenty miles south of Trent.

12–19 According to legend, Pasiphaë, wife of King Minos of Crete, was seized by a passion for a snow-white bull. The artisan Daedalus built her a wooden cow covered with cowhide and placed it over her. The bull mounted the "counterfeit" cow, and from this intercourse Pasiphaë later gave birth to the Minotaur. The Minotaur was kept in a labyrinth constructed by Daedalus. Every year it devoured a tribute of seven young men and seven young women whom Minos extracted from the Athenians in satisfaction for their murder of his son. The monster was eventually slain by Theseus with the assistance of Ariadne—Minos' daughter by Pasiphaë—who supplied him with a sword and a ball of twine.

22–26 Dante imagines the Minotaur as having a bull's body and a human head, rather than a human body and a bull's head, in accordance with other traditions.

35–37 Christ descended into Limbo soon after the earthquake said to have occurred at the moment of His death on the Cross. As Singleton points out, "Virgil, being a pagan, understands such matters dimly, at best."

41–43 Again Singleton suggests the reference here is to Empedocles' theory of the alternative supremacy of love and hate as the cause of periodic destruction and construction in the scheme of the universe.

57 *centaurs:* mythical creatures—half-horse, half-man—notorious for their gluttony and violence.

66 Saturn, enamored of Philyra and fearing the jealousy of his wife, Rhea, changed himself into a horse and in this shape begat Chiron. Chiron educated Achilles, Aesculapius, Hercules, and many other famous Greeks.

68–70 *Deianira:* the wife of Hercules, whose death she unwittingly caused. Hercules killed the centaur Nessus with a poisoned arrow for having attempted to violate her.

72 Pholus, entertaining Hercules during the latter's expedition, met his death by accidentally dropping one of his guest's poisoned arrows on his own foot.

108 Alexander the Great of Macedonia (356–323 B.C.), or Alexander of Pherae, a tyrant of Thessaly (ruled ca. 368–359 B.C.); Dionysius the Elder, tyrant of Syracuse (ruled 405–367 B.C.).

110 *Azzolino:* Ezzelino III da Romano (1194–1259), son-in-law of Emperor Frederick II and chief of the Ghibellines in Upper Italy—"one of the most cruel and feared tyrants in Christendom. He did away with large numbers of the citizens of Padua, and he put out the eyes of even the best and most noble in great numbers. . . . He caused many others to die by various tortures and torments and at one time had eleven thousand Paduans burned . . ."

111 *Obizzo II d'Este* (1247–1293): As Lord of Ferrara and later of Modena and Reggio, he was an ardent Guelph and a supporter of Charles Anjou. He is said to have wielded his power with pitiless cruelty. Obizzo was succeeded by his son Azzo VIII, by whom he was commonly supposed to have been smothered.

118–20 *That one:* Guy de Montfort (1243–1298), son of Simon de Montfort, earl of Leicester, and Eleanor, daughter of King John of England. In revenge for his father's death and for the indignities offered his corpse, Guy murdered his first cousin, Prince Henry of Cornwall, in the church of San Silvestro at Viterbo in March 1271 during the elevation of the Host, when Henry was on his knees. The heart of Prince Henry was brought to England and interred.

132 *Attila:* known as the "scourge of God." This king of the Huns (lived ca. 406–53)

ravaged both the eastern and western Roman empires.

133 *Pyrrhus*: either Pyrrhus, son of Achilles, or Pyrrhus, King of Epirus (ca. 318–272 B.C.).

135–37 The two Riniers were notorious highway robbers in Dante's day in the territory between Florence and Arezzo.

CANTO XIII / Charles Wright

1–9 The Wood of the Suicides and Spendthrifts is the only vegetation in the entirety of Hell proper: It is a dense wilderness of low-growing bushes, and has no tall trees in it. The anaphora "non" sets up the inherent negation of the two sins punished herein.

8–9 *From Cecina to Cornetto*: The Tuscan Maremma is marked at its northern and southern extremes by these two towns, or river (Cecina) and town (Cornetto). The Maremma was a vast, dense wasteland.

10–15 "For here the brutish Harpies . . .": Monsters—half-bird, half-human (bird bodies with the faces of women). Aeneas and his crew are driven from the Strophades by them, who befouled their feast and prophesied their eventual hardships.

33 *Why have you broken me?*: This is the beginning of the story of Pier della Vigna, minister of the Emperor Frederick II. Of humble origin, he studied at Bologna and entered court around 1220. At the height of his power, he was Frederick's most trusted minister. Envy ("the whore . . .") eventually toppled him, and he was imprisoned and blinded. He committed suicide in prison by smashing his head against a stone wall. At the end of his speech, he professes his innocence of the charges that brought him disfavor and incarceration.

67–72 Commentators have noted how Pier, also a poet, is given here by Dante poetic language and wordplay appropriate to his calling and style.

96–108 *Minos deploys it . . .*: Having denied their bodies in life, the suicides are denied bodily form in Hell. Minos throws their souls into this *bolgia*, where they land at random and sprout. At the Last Judgment they are denied them (their bodies) again and must hang them like laundry on their own trees.

115–21 *And here were two of them . . .*: These are the Spendthrifts who did not value their earthly goods, even as the Suicides did not value their bodies. Their representatives in the wood are Lano, member of a wealthy family of Siena, and Jacopo da Santo Andrea of Padova. Both apparently squandered their wealth and most of their property. Toppo is a river ford near Arezzo where a force from Siena was routed by one from Arezzo.

129 *Then carried away . . .*: the contrapasso in operation. The person who scattered and shredded his worldly situation is scattered and shredded, over and over again, by the black she-dogs.

143 *I was of the city which changed . . .*: Florence's first patron was Mars; thus, his "art" is warfare. Her second patron was John the Baptist. Commentators are unsure of whom this Florentine suicide actually is. Perhaps he stands for Florence herself.

CANTO XIV / Charles Wright

15 Cato the Younger (95–46 B.C.) crossed the Libyan desert a year before his death; thus, the comparison between the sand plain of the Seventh Circle and the hot desert.

16 *O vengeance of God . . .*: the rain of fire, the contrapasso, meted out by God, to whom violence has been done by those punished here.

22–24 *Flat on their backs . . .*: the three groups mentioned here—Blasphemers, Usurers, and Sodomites.

30 *Like snowflakes that fall . . .*: See Guido Cavalcanti's sonnet "Biltà di donna" ('e bianca neve scender senza venti').

31 *Or like the flames that Alexander saw*: Albertus Magnus, in *De meteoris*, tells the story of Alexander in India, where he encountered a heavy snowfall and, later, a rain of fire. Alexander had his soldiers trample the snow, apparently, but Albertus and Dante both confuse the two and have the soldiers stamping out the fire.

44–45 the rebel angels of Canto IX who barred the way into the City of Dis.

51–60 *That which I was in life . . .*: The blasphemer is Capaneus, one of the seven Kings who assaulted Thebes. Scaling the walls, he blasphemed against Jove, who struck him with a thunderbolt. Mongibello is the name for Mt. Etna, which is supposed to be Vulcan's furnace.

69 *Thebes*: a city in Boeotia where a great battle took place over its sovereignty between the two sons of Oedipus, Polynices and Eteocles. Polynices sided with the seven kings who assaulted the city, hence the Seven Against Thebes.

79–80 The Bulicame refers to a famous sulfur hot springs near Viterbo. Prostitutes supplied water in their house baths by diverting the water flow.

94–119 *In the middle of the ocean . . .*: The island of Crete is given as the source of all the waterworks of Hell. Crete was the birthplace of Trojan civilization and the center of the known world. Mt. Ida was where Rhea took her infant son, Jupiter, to protect him from his father, Saturn, who had the habit of devouring his sons when they were born. Dante places, inside Mt. Ida, the Old Man of Crete, perhaps the most elaborate symbol in Hell, and the source of the waterworks. He stands with his back to the East (Damietta), facing Rome. His golden head represents the Golden Age of man, before the Fall. The silver, brass, and iron represent the three declining ages. The clay foot, some have said, may symbolize the Church. The tears that issue from the fissure that runs through all the body but the gold eventually form the rivers of Hell, as we have seen.

134 *Phlegethon*: a river of fire in the underworld, which Dante should be able to recognize by its heat.

136 Lethe is placed by Dante atop Purgatory, in the Earthly Paradise. The souls pass through it and forget their earthly concerns on their way to Paradise, beyond the stars.

CANTO XV / *Richard Howard*

A note on form: Though aware of the axiological interest of Dante's stanzas, which so masterfully level out any and every episode into a prescribed set, I wanted to generate a text responsive to a myth of *composition*, the masonry of those irregular units of thinking and telling which the original so deftly plasters over. Thus disposed, the English verses might then correspond to another interest, that of reading the poem as a pensive narrative.

5-7 These geographical comparisons are not accidental; as Musa suggests, the northern commercial cities had a reputation for sodomy in Dante's time, as did the university city of Padua.

9 The Builder is God.

25 *Ser Brunetto:* Dante's tone of reverence and affection for the Florentine Guelph (1220–1294) known for his books, particularly the *Livres du Trésor,* an encyclopedic work written in French prose during Latini's six-year exile in France, is particularly noteworthy since he alone charges Latini with the sin of sodomy. The sodomites are doomed to an eternal wandering, comparable to the movement of the lustful in Canto V, blown about aimlessly by a wind.

45 *a gorge:* the dark wood of Canto I.

55-70 The survivors of Caesar's siege of Fiesole founded Florence. Brunetto's prophecies about Florence continues political themes begun in Cantos XIII and XIV.

76 *eternal life:* Dante expresses gratitude to Brunetto for teaching him how to become immortal through literary accomplishments.

80-81 Beatrice is referred to as the one who will reveal to the Pilgrim his future course.

98 *Priscian:* a sixth-century Roman grammarian, or perhaps a thirteenth-century Bolognese professor.

99 *Francesco d'Accorso:* a celebrated Florentine lawyer who taught law at Bologna and at Oxford.

101 *the man the pope transferred:* This refers to Andrea de' Mozzi, Bishop of Florence from 1287 to 1295, whose sodomy Dante emphasizes in his reference to "abused flesh."

CANTO XVI / *Richard Howard*

32 *the good Gualdrada:* a lady known for her beauty, wit, and modesty, married to Guido Guerra IV. The wisdom of her grandson, mentioned in line 33 with regard to "strategy and sword," is exemplified by his advice to the Florentines not to undertake a campaign against Siena in 1260; they ignored his words and the battle destroyed the Guelph party in Florence.

36 *Tegghiaio Aldobrandini:* Like Guido Guerra, a leader of the Guelph party in Florence, who also tried to dissuade the Guelphs from attacking the Sienese; the fact that his advice was disregarded accounts for Dante's saying "the world should have heeded" his voice.

38-39 *Jacopo Rusticucci:* a Florentine of humble birth who became a prominent citizen. He was said to have turned to the vice of sodomy because his wife was impossible to live with.

55 *the very center:* the center of the earth, and consequently the lowest part of Hell.

61 Little is known of Guglielmo Borsiere save that he died, evidently, about 1300. Boccaccio says he was a knight of the court and a peacemaker.

64-67 Dante's rhetorical condemnation of Florence may be linked with other political prophecies in Cantos XIII and XIV, as well as with Brunetto Latini's words in Canto XV. All suggest the decay of the city through personal squandering of the gifts of God.

94 *I had a cord:* Suddenly introduced, this cord, which probably represents fallacious

self-confidence (for with it Dante had thought to catch the leopard mentioned in Canto I), is disposed of by Dante's guide (Reason) to indicate that henceforth the Pilgrim will rely on Virgil alone, especially in contending with Fraud, personified by the monster Geryon, which appears at the canto's end.

CANTO XVII / *Stanley Plumly*

1 *Geryon:* emblem of fraud, he is Dante's pagan/Christian composite: In classical mythology he is a kingly and giant triple-shaped creature (three heads or three bodies) whom Hercules, in line with his labors, must kill in order to acquire the monster's flocks and herds. Geryon is also sometimes seen as a robber and murderer who lures the unwary. In Revelations: "their faces were as the faces of men . . . and they had tails like unto scorpions." Dante wants a creature with a vulnerable human face, a reptile's grotesque body (and tail), and an ancient bird's (a kind of pterodactyl) creaking gift of flight. The huge paws and arms add menace.

16 *Turks . . . Tartars:* skilled medieval weavers.

18 *Arachne:* Famous for her weaving, she was punished for her hubris in challenging Minerva to a contest; and thus turned into a spider.

21 *the beaver:* Not unlike Geryon, the beaver was believed to have magical powers in its tail, capable of deluding and captivating fish.

22 *Germans:* infamous heavy drinkers, from antiquity on.

30 *descending to our right:* Much is made by Sinclair and others of the "rare right turns" in Hell. Perhaps it is a moral point. Or perhaps all turns in *The Inferno,* left or right, should be seen as part of the configuration of the many circles within circles that dominates the structural imagination of the poets' journey.

53 *Coat-of-arms:* for different Florentine and Paduan families famous for usury.

63 Mandelbaum identifies this usurer—the anonymous speaker here—as Reginaldo Scrovegni, whose sins were great enough that his son built Scrovegni Chapel in atonement.

65 *Vitaliano:* According to Mandelbaum, this is probably Vitaliano del Dente of Padua, a chief magistrate of Vicenza.

69 *Soldier:* Actually, "cavalier" is literally closer to the original, though Dante sees this soldier of fortune—the esteemed Florentine banker Giovanni Buiamonte—as even more guilty than his fellow usurers, since he holds high public office. The "purse of goats" (three black goats) refers to the coat-of-arms of the Becchi family, of which Buiamonte was a member.

79 *quartan fear:* This refers to quartan fever, a serious ague with symptoms not unlike malaria.

95 *Phaethon:* son of Apollo, he could not control the horses when given the chance to drive his father's chariot. The riot almost set the earth on fire. The punishment was death by thunderbolt.

98 *Icarus:* another son who failed to heed the warning, and so flew too close to the source with his father's wings of wax.

115 *The falcon:* A falcon will fly into exhaustion until it finds its prey or is called back.

CANTO XVIII / *Stanley Plumly*

2 *Malebolge:* the Eighth Circle: of "evil-pouches" or ditches, which amount to ten concentric trenches, each representing the valley of a different type of fraud, descending—somewhat in the manner of an amphitheater—to a common pit.

25 *Jubilee:* refers to the Holy Year of 1300, proclaimed so by Pope Boniface VIII for the purpose of granting indulgences. So many pilgrims showed up for their sin reductions that movement across the bridge to St. Peter's had to be controlled. The flow of two-way traffic across Ponte S'Angelo meant that while some eyes looked to St. Peter's, other eyes, moving in the opposite direction, looked at Mt. Giordano.

46 The extremity of Venedico Coccianemico's sin is that he was said to have procured his own sister for services to the Marquis of Este.

51 *Ghisolabella: "la bella."*

56 *Sipa:* This is dialect for "yes," as spoken in the countryside and towns between the Bologna border rivers Savena and Reno. As suggested by Sinclair: There are more Bolognese here in Hell than in Bologna. More *si*-sayers, anyway.

79 As leader of the Argonauts, Jason set a bad example. On their way to Colchis to secure the Golden Fleece, he and his men stopped off at the strange isle of Lemnos, where Jason seduced and left pregnant Hypsipyle. Hypsipyle's virtue was that she had saved her father from the fate of all the other men on the island, whose women had killed them. As for Jason—yet another example of the abuse of power —he had earlier abandoned Medea, whose revenge was to kill their two children. So he has suffered punishment on earth as well.

104 *their excrement:* Human waste has nearly the worst odor of all animal waste.

113 *Allessio Interminei:* another member of a prominent family—the Guelphs of Lucca.

123 *Thais:* a character, a courtesan, in the *Eunuchus* by Terence, who may or may not be, according to Mandelbaum, the "fulsome flatterer" Dante makes her out to be. Dante may be taking his cue from Cicero's commentary on the play.

CANTO XIX / *C. K. Williams*

A note on form: I'm always struck by the firmness of Dante's stanzas, how each is like a block of stone in an edifice, with the rhyme emphasizing this irrevocable solidity. Given that I wanted as little divergence from Dante's meaning as far as I could make it out, that I wanted to keep a strong stanza, with no run-ons except where they occur in the original, and that I wanted each stanza to have at least one full rhyme (though I didn't think I could keep the linkings of the terza rima without too much distortion), I decided I needed a supple line to make the stanzas, and so arrived at what I have here, which, halfway through, I realized, not to my surprise, were the line and stanza Elizabeth Bishop used in "The Moose," one of the contemporary poems I most admire.

1 *Simon Magus:* Simon of Samaria, a sorcerer, who, after his conversion by Philip (Acts 8:9–24), tried to purchase the power of conferring the Holy Ghost. Peter rebuked him. "Your money go with you to damnation, because you thought God's gift was for sale." From his name comes the term "simony," the crime of buying or selling ecclesiastical offices or sacraments. Dante felt particularly strongly about

the part simony played in the corruption of the church, and about its debasing moral and political effects.

36 *San Giovanni*: the baptistery of the present cathedral in Florence. In Dante's time, it was the main church of Florence; Dante was baptized in it.

39 The story of Dante's breaking a baptismal font to save someone (supposedly a child) from drowning is known only from Dante's report here. Dante seems to be trying to clear up a misinterpretation of the event which had defamed him in some way.

90 Nicholas III, who was pope from 1277 to 1280. He was of the Orsini family of Rome; hence the "bear" and the "cubs" referred to in lines 139–144.

98 Paid assassins were executed in Florence by being placed head down in a pit, which was then filled with dirt. This gruesome punishment is the source of the image Dante uses for the divine retribution against the Simonists.

104 Nicholas thinks that Dante is Boniface VIII, the pope who succeeded him. The souls in Hell know the future, and since Boniface didn't die until 1303, Dante uses the device of Nicholas' surprise to regale Boniface—Cardinal Benedetto Caetani—whom Dante particularly detested.

111 The "lovely lady" is the Church.

168 This is Clement V, pope from 1305–1314. He contrived with King Philip IV of France to move the papacy from Rome to Avignon, the so-called "Babylonian Captivity," which lasted until 1377.

169 *Jason*: In 2 Maccabees 4.7f, Jason bribed King Antiochus of Syria into bestowing on him the office of High Priest of the Jews. Clement was reputed to have bribed Philip as part of the conniving by which he was made pope.

191–92 *The betraying soul*: Judas Iscariot, whom Matthias replaced among the twelve disciples.

198 Dante believed, although there seems to be no historical evidence to the effect, that Nicholas was bribed by the Emperor Palaeologus to conspire against Charles I of Anjou, who was subsequently ousted from the kingdom of Sicily.

202 *those great keys*: the symbol of the papacy, which Dante still supported, despite his rage at the corrupt popes.

211 See Revelations XVII for "the whore that sitteth upon many waters." "The Evangelist" would be John of Patmos, author of the Book of Revelations. In 216ff., the "seven heads" symbolize the seven gifts of the holy spirit; the "ten horns" the Ten Commandments. "Her consort" is the papacy.

229 This refers to "The Donation of Constantine," a legend current in Dante's time but subsequently proven spurious, which said that Constantine, when he transferred the seat of Empire from Rome to Byzantium at the time of his conversion, donated the western part of the Roman Empire, with its great wealth, to the Church. "The first rich father" was the pope at that time, Sylvester I.

CANTO XX / *Robert Pinsky*

15 The souls condemned here practiced occult arts to see the future; as punishment for this impiety they must look backward.

34 *Amphiaraus*: one of the seven kings who fought against Thebes. He foresaw his own

death in battle, and tried to avert it by fleeing, but was swallowed by an earth-quake while running away.

39–43 *Tiresias:* the soothsayer of Thebes. He was transformed to a woman when he struck a pair of copulating snakes with his staff. Seven years later he was changed back to a man by again striking at coupled snakes.

44 *Aruns:* an Etruscan soothsayer from near Carrara, the source of white marble. He supposedly predicted the civil war and Caesar's victory.

51 *Manto:* the daughter of Tiresias and a prophetess. She was supposed to have come to Italy.

60–62 On this island in Lake Garda the three church jurisdictions of Trentino, Brescia, and Verona meet.

81–82 After Alberto da Casalodi became lord of Mantua in 1272, he followed the advice of Pinamonte dei Buonaccorsi to win over his opposition by banishing his sup-porters. When the nobles favoring Casalodi were in exile, Pinamonte seized power.

92–93 The males of Greece were away at the Trojan War.

94–96 *Calchas:* the augur who chose the most auspicious moment for the Greek ships to sail from Aulis for Troy. *Eurypylus:* another soothsayer among the Greek expedition.

97 Michael Scot, or Scotto (ca. 1175–1235), was a Scottish scholar, astrologer, and occult-ist believed to have served as court astrologer to Frederick II at Palermo.

99 *Guido Bonatti:* a thirteenth-century astrologer, author of a treatise on astronomy. *Asdente:* Italian for "Toothless." This was the nickname of Maestro Benvenuto, a shoemaker of Parma who was known as a prophet and soothsayer.

105 Italian folklore sees the spots on the moon as the shape of Cain carrying thorns; in this legend, he was banished to the moon by God after trying to excuse himself for murdering his brother Abel.

CANTO XXI / *Susan Mitchell*

1–2 This is one of several places in the *Inferno* (see also *Inf* IV, 103–05, and VII, 112) where Dante alludes to conversations that the reader is not permitted to hear. This is also one of several places in the *Inferno* where Dante links talking with walking. In fact, the poem's iambic pentameter seems to grow out of the rhythms of walking, while the breath units of the lines are affected by the steep inclines, the high banks, and cliffs, which leave the poet so short of breath in Canto XXIV, lines 43–45, that he has to sit down and rest.

37 The group name for the devils, "Evil Claws," singles out their most terrifying feature: sharp claws, like the talons of birds of prey, which the devils are quick to use on sinners who emerge from the boiling pitch. The devils' pitchforks and grappling hooks are a refinement or technological improvement of a natural part of demon anatomy.

38 *Saint Zita:* the patron saint of Lucca. She is entombed in that city's Church of San Frediano. Not officially canonized until 1690, she was nevertheless venerated in Dante's time.

41 *Except for Bonturo:* a phrase that has to be understood as sarcastic. Bonturo Date, the political boss of Lucca, was notorious for taking bribes and stands out as unusually corrupt in a city that was known for corruption.

48 The Holy Face or Santo Volto was a very ancient image of Christ made of dark wood. This religious object is still greatly venerated and can be seen in the nave of the cathedral of San Martino at Lucca. Since the Lucchese prayed to the Holy Face when they were in serious trouble, the devils' taunt means that the sinner cannot expect help where he is now. But the devils, in their vulgar way, are also implying that the sinner's rear end, black with pitch, resembles the dark wood of the ancient crucifix, and as a holy object, it would, of course, have no place in Hell.

50 *The Serchio:* a stream near Lucca, known for its pure, clear water, where the Lucchese often bathed in summer.

106–11 The devil is telling the truth when he says that the bridge has been smashed, but he deliberately misinforms Virgil when he gives him directions for getting around the impasse. However, that lie will not be discovered until Canto XXIII, lines 116–17.

114 What shattered the roadway was the earthquake that followed Christ's death on the Cross and announced his entry into Hell. According to William Langland's fourteenth-century account in *Piers Plowman*, when Christ died "Daylight shrank in terror; the sun was darkened. Walls stirred from their bases and split asunder. A shudder ran through the whole wide world" (tr. A.V.C. Schmidt; Oxford University Press, 1992, p. 212). That shudder caused the collapse of the bridges of Hell. Virgil only now learns about this collapse because his last visit to Hell occurred before Christ's death.

118–23 Translators fall into two groups when it comes to handling the names of the devils. Some preserve the Italian names, but this is an advantage only to a reader knowledgeable enough to recognize in the devils' names comic allusions to real Italian families living in Dante's time—the Malabranca in Rome and the Raffacani in Florence, for example. Others translate the names into English, but literal translations lose the coarse vigor of the Italian names, and the meanings of a few names can only be guessed at. In my own translations, I have tried to be true to a folklore tradition that emphasizes the crudeness and sheer nastiness of the devils. The devils exhibit a wild animal energy in keeping with their claws, snouts, tails, and in one case, tusks; and their names call attention to their animality.

CANTO XXII / *Susan Mitchell*

4 At the Battle of Campaldino on June 11, 1289, Dante would have seen the Aretine Ghibellines, the forces of Arezzo, defeated by the Guelph Florentines.

48 This sinner is never named, though according to early commentators he was Ciampolo or Gian Paolo. The region he was from, Navarre, was a part of the western Pyrenees, now dividing Spain and France.

52 Thibaut II, King of Navarre from 1253 to 1270, was known for his justice and clemency.

81 *Fra Gomita:* a Sardinian friar. She was appointed chancellor of Nino Visconti of Pisa, a judge of the judicial district of Gallura in Sardinia. He was notorious for accepting bribes, though Nino overlooked his corruption until Gomita was bribed into letting several of Nino's prisoners escape. When Nino learned of this, he had Fra Gomita hanged.

88 *Don Michele Zanche:* replaced Fra Gomita as Nino Visconti's chancellor, and his reputation for accepting bribes was even worse than his predecessor's. He was involved in various intrigues and attempts to gain political power and in 1275 he was murdered by his son-in-law, Branca d'Oria. In Canto XXX, Dante will discover that Branca d'Oria's soul is already in Hell, even though his body goes about its everyday affairs on earth.

CANTO XXIII / *Carolyn Forché*

2 The order is that of the Franciscan brothers, referred to as the Friars Minor, or lesser order.
4 In Aesop's fable, the frog tricks the mouse by offering to bear it across the river with the secret intention of pulling the mouse to the bottom. As the frog attempts this, the frog is snatched by a hawk. In versions compatible with my reading of Dante's allegorical use of the fable, the mouse escapes.
14 The Malebranch (or Evil Talons) are black, winged creatures who appear in Canto XXI; they threaten Virgil and Dante, who escape, pursued by them.
16 Mirrors were then backed by lead.
39 The monks of Cluny wore amply cut, elegant robes. This may also refer to an incident in Cologne, where monks purportedly once requested to wear red robes decorated with silver and, as punishment for this vanity, were forced to wear more amply cut robes of ordinary fabric.
43 Legend has it that Frederick II punished traitors by cloaking them in lead and throwing them into boiling caldrons.
71 The town on the Arno is Florence.
79 The "Jovial Friars" were the *Ordo militiae beatae Mariae*, founded in 1261. These Knights of St. Mary, a religious order of clergymen and laymen, were charged with keeping the peace among political factions and defending the oppressed. Loderingo degli Andalo, a Ghibelline, founded the order. His joint tenure with Catalano, a Guelph, failed, and violence ensued. Gardingo was the area around Florence where the Ghibelline family lived. Their houses were destroyed in the fighting.
84 The palace at Gardingo was sacked and burned.
85 *a crucified man:* Caiaphas.
93 The one man was Jesus of Nazareth.
100 Virgil hadn't seen Caiaphas on his first journey through Hell, and that journey was made before the birth of Christ.

CANTO XXIV / *Carolyn Forché*

2 The sun is in Aquarius from January 21 to February 21.
6 Hoarfrost melts rapidly.
34 *Malebolge:* the region of Hell.
48 This may refer beyond the immediate climb, to the ascent into Purgatory that lies ahead.
76 The Libyan desert is from Lucan's *Pharsalia.*
84 *heliotrope:* a stone with powers to make one invisible.

98 The details of the Phoenix legend are from Ovid (*Metamorphosis*, XV, 392–407). After living for five hundred years, the nest of the Phoenix catches fire. The Phoenix dies and is reborn from its own ashes.

103 Possibly refers to epilepsy.

116 Vanni Fucci was a ruffian who stole the treasure of San Jacopo from the Church of San Zeno. An innocent man, Rampino dei Foresi, was arrested, but Vanni Fucci blamed the receiver of the goods, who was hanged, while Rampino went free.

117 *Pistoia*: the village that was the site of the feud between members of the Black Party and the White Party.

130 Vanni Fucci prophesies these events: In 1301 members of the Black Party of Pistoia were expelled and their houses burned; under Charles of Valois, the Blacks of Pistoia and Florence were able to renew their attacks on the White Party, whom they expelled in 1302. The description of the battle is metaphorical. Mars, the god of War, draws forth a vapor whose fiery nature will enter into conflict with the watery clouds around it, causing thunder and lightning. This is in keeping with the meteorology of the time. The defeat of the Whites takes place at Campo Piceno, a name for the plain of Pistoia.

CANTO XXV / *Richard Wilbur*

Dante and Virgil are still in the Seventh Chasm, to which the souls of thieves are assigned. As Canto XXIV has shown, it is a dark place, and full of reptiles that variously punish the sinners—twining around them so as to bind their thievish hands, or (as happened to Vanni Fucci in XXIV, 97ff.) causing them to burn to ashes and then re-form. What first occurs in Canto XXV is that Vanni Fucci, at the conclusion of a prophecy grievous to Dante, makes a gesture of obscene defiance toward God, is therefore throttled and bound by serpents, and flees, pursued by the centaur Cacus. The remainder of the canto is concerned with the transformations undergone by five thieves of Florence, all of noble family, who have been identified as Agnello de' Brunelleschi Buoso (degli Abati?), Puccio "Sciancato" de' Galigai, Cianfa de' Donati, and Francesco de' Cavalcanti. Cianfa, who has been changed into a six-footed serpent, attacks Agnello and merges with him to create a monster that is neither reptile nor man. Then Francesco, who is temporarily a small reptile, assaults Buoso and exchanges shapes with him, the man becoming a *serpentello* and the reptile becoming a man. Puccio remains unchanged, but for the moment only. The logic of these painful transformations is that the thieves, who in life appropriated what was not theirs, are here punished by the repeated loss even of their own persons.

2 *made figs*: This insulting gesture, which has not gone out of fashion, is made by closing the hand into a fist with the thumb protruding between the index and second fingers.

12 *the base begetters*: Pistoia, Vanni Fucci's home town, was thought to have been settled by the survivors of Catiline's army.

15 *not him*: This is Capaneus, another proud blasphemer, who has appeared earlier, in Canto XIV, 46ff.

18 *that half-cooked sinner*: In Italian, the word is *acerbo*, meaning green, bitter, unripe.

Singleton points out that both Capaneus and Fucci are proud spirits being pun-
ished by fire—one by a rain of fire that does not "ripen" him (Canto XIV, line 48),
the other by the breath of Cacus' dragon. ". . . in both cases the proud sinner is
'ripened' (humbled) by fire for his blasphemy" (Singleton, 430–31).

19 *Maremma*: a marshy coastal area in Tuscany, noted in Dante's day for malaria and
for its snake population.

25 *Cacus*: According to Dante's classical sources, this voracious monster, a fire-breath-
ing son of Vulcan, dwelt in a cave on the Aventine. He stole some of the cattle that
Hercules had taken from the monster Geryon, and for this Hercules slew him.
Perhaps because Virgil's account of Cacus (*Aeneid* VIII, 193ff.) described the crea-
ture as "half-human," Dante was led to imagine Cacus as a centaur, and to transfer
his fire-breathing attribute to a dragon borne upon his shoulders. It is because of
his theft of Hercules' cattle that Cacus is here among the thieves and not with "his
brothers," the centaurs who guard the violent in Canto XII.

35 *three spirits*: Agnello, Buoso, and Puccio.

43 *Where's Cianfa?*: Unbeknownst to the three companions, Cianfa has been waylaid
and changed into a six-footed serpent that will, in a few lines, appear and attack
Agnello.

83 *a little reptile*: This form houses, for the present, the soul of Francesco.

85 *one of them*: Buoso.

85–86 *the spot/ through which our earliest nourishment must come*: the navel.

94ff. Lucan's *Pharsalia* (IX, 763–76, 790–97) tells how the Roman soldier Sabellus,
bitten by a serpent in the Libyan desert, was changed into a "pool of corruption,"
and how the soldier Nasidius, similarly poisoned, swelled up "till all shape was
lost." Ovid tells of the famous transformations of Cadmus and Arethusa in his
Metamorphoses (IV, 576–80, 586–89; V, 572–641).

116 *that member*: the penis.

117 *branched then into two*: "In these animals [lizards] there are two penes." *Encyclo-
paedia Britannica*, 11th Edition, "Reproductive System."

136 *the soul that had become a beast*: Buoso.

137 *the other*: Francesco.

139–40 *the one/ who lingered*: Puccio.

151 *Gaville*: Francesco de' Cavalcanti was killed by some citizens of Gaville, a town in
the upper Val d'Arno; his kinsmen bloodily avenged him, and therefore Gaville is
said to weep on Francesco's account.

CANTO XXVI / *W. S. Merwin*

9 Perhaps in part to evoke the elusive style of prophetic utterances, the allusion here is
full of possible interpretations but points clearly to no single, unequivocal object.
The probable references are these: Prato is a Tuscan town between Florence and
Pistoia. Smaller than Florence, it remained, in general, on good terms with the
larger state, though the allusion here may suggest an ancient jealousy, or a long-
restrained resentment at Florentine arrogance. But it seems more likely that the
primary reference is to Cardinal Niccolò da Prato, who had tried to pacify the
bitter factions in Florence, had failed, and in June of 1304 had left Florence in

disgust, excommunicating its inhabitants. The misfortunes to which Dante's "prophecy" refers were attributed to the Cardinal's imprecation.

They include a catastrophe at the new Ponte alla Carraia over the Arno, where many spectators had gathered, as Benvenuto wrote, after "the people of the St. Florian quarter had it publicly proclaimed that whoever wanted to have news of the other world should come to the Ponte alla Carraia at the beginning of May. They set up floats on boats and barges and arranged a sort of representation of Hell, with fires and other pains and torments . . . everyone went to see it . . . Because of that, the Ponte alla Carraia, which was then made of wood . . . crashed into the Arno with all the people on it . . ." and a great many were killed. A while later a fire in the city destroyed over seventeen hundred buildings, including towers and palazzi. I cannot resolve what seems to me a confusion in the chronology. The Cardinal left in June, and if the Ponte alla Carraia collapsed in May of the same year, as Charles Singleton, citing Villari's *Cronica*, tells us, then the curse must have come after the event.

A consideration of the chronology suggests another reason for Dante's putting the dire happenings in the form of a veiled prophecy. If the disasters mentioned above are among those referred to, they took place several years after 1300, the "Ideal Date of Vision" of the *Commedia*.

34 Kings II, 2:23–24:

"And Eliseus went up from thence to Bethel. And as he was going up by the way, little boys came out of the city and mocked him, saying: Go up, thou bald head. Go up, thou bald head.

"And looking back, he saw them, and cursed them in the name of the Lord, and there came forth two bears out of the forest, and tore of them two and forty boys."

35 Kings II 2:11–12:

"And as they went on, walking and talking together, behold a fiery chariot, and fiery horses parted them both asunder, and Elias went up by a whirlwind into heaven."

54 Eteocles and Polynices were twin sons of Oedipus and Jocasta. They forced Oedipus to abdicate and leave Thebes, and he prayed that enmity should divide them forever. They agreed to rule Thebes alternately, each one for a year at a time. But Eteocles, at the end of his reign, refused to relinquish the kingdom, and the civil war that led to the Seven Against Thebes broke out. The brothers killed each other in single combat. Their bodies were placed on one pyre, but as the flame rose it split apart.

56 The person of Ulysses, in whatever setting, surely needs no general identification. But it is worth noting that Diomed, or Diomedes, King of Argos and one of the heroes who was with Ulysses in the war against Troy, was his accomplice in luring Achilles into that war, and in the tactic that led to the capture of the Palladium, the image of Pallas Athene that protected Troy. And Dante appears to have assumed that Diomedes was also a party to Ulysses' famous stratagem of the wooden horse, which led to the sack of Troy. But it should be remembered, in regard both to this and to Dante's account of Ulysses' final voyage, that Dante did not know the Odyssey, but only later references to Ulysses. On the other hand, we know and can suppose that Dante knew that two Genoese brothers named Vivaldi, in 1291,

sailed through the Straits of Gibraltar, westward, looking for India, and never returned—and the Americas were spared thus for another two centuries.

62 *Deidamia*: Achilles' wife.

91 *Circe*: sorceress who transformed men into swine.

92 *Gaeta*: seaport in southern Italy named for Aeneas' nurse.

103–09 an itinerary more imaginary than literal. Spain and Morocco of course are far to the west of Sardinia. At the Straits of Gibraltar, the Pillars of Hercules, according to the tradition, were once a single mountain until they were torn apart by that sun hero. During the later Middle Ages they were taken to represent the western limits of human enterprise, beyond which no one could presume to travel and live to tell of it.

CANTO XXVII / *W. S. Merwin*

7–12 Phalaris, a tyrant of Agrigentum in Sicily, had his victims locked into a brazen image of a bull, which was then roasted. The shrieks of the victim, it is said, were like the bellowing of a bull. Perillus, the inventor of the device, was supposedly its first victim.

19–20 This unnamed voice reduced to asking for news of home is Guido da Montefeltro, once known as "The Fox," a brilliant and often successful military leader of the Ghibelline faction, from Romagna. He was excommunicated for returning from exile, to which he had been sentenced by the Vatican. Eventually he left secular life altogether and in 1296 joined the Franciscan order. But according to tradition, in 1298 Pope Boniface VIII persuaded him to tell how the citadel of Palestrina could be taken, and Guido's advice on that occasion is the basis for Dante's finding him here among the authors of covert operations and fraudulent counsel.

40–51 There are references throughout to municipalities and ruling families of Romagna.

52 On the river Savio, between Forlí and Rimini, at the foothills of the Apennines, the municipality of Cesena.

56 Guido's advice, according to Riccobaldo, chronicler of Ferrara, was to "promise much and fulfill little"—a practice so generally assumed among those engaged in politics that it seems there must have been something more remarkable and specific which has remained a secret.

86 the war between Pope Boniface VIII and the Colonna family, who contested the succession that had led to the Pope's position, and maintained that it was based upon fraud. "Lateran" here refers to Rome itself.

89 *Acre*: from the French St. Jean d'Acre, and Old Testament Accho; a seaport now part of Israel, northwest of Jerusalem. The Crusaders took it in 1104 and it was their principal port for eighty-three years. Saladin recaptured it. In 1191 Richard Coeur de Lion and Philip Augustus of France led the campaign that took the port again and it remained in Christian hands for a century after that. In 1294 it was taken back by a sultan, thus ending the western kingdom of Jerusalem.

94 In the legend recounted by Jacobus de Varagine, archbishop of Genoa from 1292 to 1298, Constantine, as a punishment for persecuting Christians, contracted leprosy.

The pagan clergy prescribed a bath in infants' blood. Three thousand babies were brought in, but the shrieks of lamentation touched Constantine and he said he would rather die than butcher these innocents. That night Saints Peter and Paul appeared to him and told him to consult a certain Sylvester, who was living in a cave on Mt. Socrate. Sylvester, in due course, baptized Constantine, who was cured on the spot. Constantine went back and converted his mother, and between them they brought about the Christianization of Rome.

102 *Penestrino:* now Palestrina, the citadel of the Colonna family, some twenty miles southeast of Rome. In 1298, when the Colonnas surrendered to Pope Boniface VIII, who had promised them amnesty, the Pope completely destroyed the city.

124 *Minos:* guardian, at the entrance to the Second Circle of Hell, who hears the offenses of those who come before him, and assigns them to their eternal places in the abyss.

CANTO XXVIII / *Robert Pinsky*

7 Though modern Apulia is the southeast heel of the peninsula, on the Adriatic coast, in the Middle Ages the name indicated the whole of southern Italy, the locale of the bloodshed listed in the following lines.

11–12 According to Livy's *History*, Hannibal brought home to Carthage a heap of gold rings taken from the fingers of slain Romans, as proof of his victory over them.

14 *Robert Guiscard:* (1015–1085), a Norman adventurer and warrior, Duke of Apulia and Calabria.

15 *At Ceperano:* where Apulian barons were pledged to defend the pass on behalf of Manfred, natural son of Frederick II, they instead admitted the troops of Charles of Anjou, leading to the death of Manfred in 1266.

18 *Near Tagliacozzo:* where Alardo de Valery devised the strategy by which Charles of Anjou defeated Manfred's nephew in 1268.

30 Apparently, Dante and his contemporaries believed that Mohammed was a renegade cardinal. This divergence from historical truth amounts to the invention of an imaginary character, which the translator here indicates by retaining the Italian "Maömetto."

32 *Ali:* Mohammed's nephew, son-in-law, and devoted follower.

53 Fra Dolcino Tornielli of Novara was head of the reformist Apostolic Brothers, a group opposed to the temporal power of the clergy and accused of heretical practices, including the communal sharing of goods and of women. After taking refuge in the mountains, Fra Dolcino and his followers were besieged and starved out. Dolcino and his alleged mistress were burned alive in 1307.

70 *Pier da Medicina:* (d. 1271?) described as a sower of discord.

71–82 Around 1215, Malatestino, Lord of Rimini, the one-eyed tyrant, invited two noblemen of Fano—Guido de Cassero and Angiolello di Carignano—to a conference at La Cattolica. Malatestino's men attacked their boat and threw them overboard in the seas near the cliff of Focara. Drowned, they had no need to pray for fair winds off that treacherous promontory.

75–76 *Neptune:* the god of the sea; Majorca and Cyprus represent the east-west breadth of the Mediterranean Sea.

92–95 Caius Curio was bribed by Caesar to betray Pompey and, according to Lucan, urged Caesar to cross the Rubicon, when he hesitated.

96–100 *Mosca de' Lamberti:* renewed the Ghibelline feud with the Guelphs in 1215 by inciting the Amidei family to murder the Guelph Buondelmonte dei Buondelmonti for breaking his engagement to one of their daughters. Later the Lamberti family was exiled from Florence.

119–27 *Bertrand de Born:* Lord of Hautefort near Périgueux. He was a soldier and troubador who died in 1215 as a Cistercian monk. King Henry II is supposed to have believed that Bertran inspired the rebellion of his son Prince Henry, the "Young King."

123–24 The biblical King David's counselor Achitophel inspired the rebellion of Absalom, David's son, against his father.

CANTO XXIX / *Alfred Corn*

For Dante's hendecasyllabic and iambic terza rima, I've substituted iambic pentameter, rhyming lines one and three of each tercet.

Less well known than many of the *canti*, XXIX has nevertheless an unfailing interest, and seems to stand behind later literary works such as the "Alchimie du Verbe" section of Rimbaud's *Une saison en enfer*, Pound's "Sestina: Altaforte," and Eliot's "The Hollow Men."

On the brink of the ninth *bolgia* (ditch or trench), Dante's own perceived affinity with the sin "punished so severely there" (strife) is suggested by his lingering behind so that Virgil has to admonish him to push on. The excuse given is that he was searching for the shade of his relative, Geri del Bello, whose death the Alighieri family never avenged. The pilgrim must put aside his last lingering guilt for having failed to participate in the vendetta required by the social code of his time.

When they reach the tenth *bolgia*, which holds the falsifiers, they brood on the fate of the alchemists. The affliction of a disease resembling leprosy can suggest the transformation worked on metal by alchemy. Appearance is altered in both cases, but the punishment makes of it a horrible metamorphosis and enlists collaboration from the guilty, who claw at each other's sores. Dante uses the occasion to launch a few barbs at the Sienese, considered foolish and vain by their contemporaries in Florence.

9 This is the first precise indication of distance in the *Commedia*. It may or may not help us map *Inferno*, but the insistence here on doubleness in the number 22 invites interpretation.

10 By Charles Singleton's reckoning, this makes it 1:00 P.M.

27 *Geri del Bello:* mentioned above, the first cousin of Dante's father. Early commentators are not agreed on all the particulars surrounding his life, but at least we know he was murdered, probably by a member of the Sacchetti family, in the late thirteenth century. At the writing of the *Commedia,* he had not been avenged; hence Dante's unresolved feelings here. One account tells that Geri's nephews did avenge him later, and there is a record of the act of reconciliation between the Alighieri and the Sacchetti in 1342, but nothing more substantial is known about the feud.

29 *Altaforte:* "Hautefort" in French, or "High Fort" in English, was the stronghold of Bertran de Born, mentioned in the previous canto, line 134. It was located in the bishopric of Périgueux, in what is now the Dordogne.

47–48 The Valdichiano, or valley of the Chiana River, is in Tuscany and leads directly into the Arno near Arezzo. It was notorious for the presence of malaria, especially in the summer. The same was true for the region of Maremma in Tuscany, and presumably for Sardinia, as well.

58–64 Legend tells how Jupiter fathered a child named Aeacus with the nymph Aegina on the island of Oenone in the Saronic Gulf off the coast of mainland Greece. Aeacus later renamed the island after his mother. Juno, hearing of the affair, afflicted its inhabitants with a plague. Only the son Aeacus survived, but he pleaded with Jupiter to restore the island's population, who did so by changing ants into men.

109 This speaker is usually identified as Griffolino, an alchemist who lived in Arezzo. The rest of the story is as told here: After Griffolino was paid to but failed to teach Albero da Siena how to fly, the latter had him sentenced as a sorcerer and burned at the stake. Albero was said by early commentators to be the son or favorite of a bishop of Siena named, appositely enough, Bonfiglio, a well-known scourge to heretics. But even the scant information available about this figure seems to contradict the identification. In any case, it is Griffolino's practice of alchemy that has condemned him to the tenth *bolgia,* not his failure at being a flight instructor.

127–28 Niccolò de' Salimbeni, according to a long tradition of commentary, was a member of the Sienese "Brigata Spendereccia" (referred to in line 130), a band of friends devoted to conspicuous expenditure. Apparently some of his extravagance involved spicing gourmet dishes with cloves, which were very costly at the time.

129 Siena, because of its vanity, is the kitchen garden where the absurd custom of using cloves could flourish.

131 Caccia d'Ascian lived in Asciano, near Siena, in the second half of the thirteenth century. He was also a member of the Spendthrift Brigade.

132 The nickname "l'Abbagliato," "Spellbound" or "Bedazzled," was given to one of the Spendthrifts usually identified as Bartolommeo de' Folcacchieri of Siena. His nickname points up the irony of praising him for his wisdom.

136 *Capocchio:* a Florentine. He was burned at the stake in 1293 as an alchemist. Tradition says that he was one of Dante's fellow students and that he was a well-known mimic of people and objects. Of course, the "alchemy" he practiced must have been a species of mimicry as well.

CANTO XXX / *Alfred Corn*

1–12 Jupiter's liaison with Semele, daughter of the Theban King Cadmus, led to the birth of Bacchus. Juno took revenge by driving Semele's brother-in-law Athamas mad so that he mistook his wife Ino (Semele's sister) for a lioness and his two sons for cubs. Dante's account of their deaths agrees substantially with Ovid's in the *Metamorphoses,* IV, 512ff.

16–21 After the Trojan defeat, Queen Hecuba was taken as a captive to Greece. She was made to witness the sacrifice of her daughter Polyxena and later saw the unburied body of her son Polydorus, killed by his uncle, the King of Thrace. Ovid says she began howling like a dog (*Metamorphoses* XIII, 568ff.)

28–31 This is the Capocchio of the previous canto (line 136) and his companion Griffolino (see Canto XXIX, lines 109–20).

32–45 *Gianni Schicchi:* one of the Cavalcanti family of Florence who lived in the late thirteenth century. Simone di Donati persuaded Gianni Schicchi to impersonate his father Buoso Donati (see Canto XXV) after the latter's death in order to make a will favorable to Simone. Gianni Schicchi disguised himself and dictated a will to the notary, following the proper form, but also put in some provisions for himself, including the bequest of the lead mare of Donati's mule herd.

37–41 *Myrrha:* the daughter of King Cinyrus of Cyprus who conceived an incestuous passion for her father and impersonated another woman in order to entice him. He discovered what she had done and was going to kill her, but she fled, only to be changed into a myrrh tree, after having given birth to Adonis (Ovid, *Metamorphoses* X, 298ff.)

61–90 *Master Adam:* may have been English; he resided in Brescia and later Bologna. Eventually he was summoned to Romena, a small town in the hilly Casentino region near Florence, by the Guidi, a noble family of the town. For them he counterfeited the gold florin of Florence, making a coin with only 21 karats of gold instead of the standard 24. The florin was always stamped with an image of John the Baptist, Florence's patron saint. Master Adam was burned at the stake by the Florentines in 1281, the normal punishment for counterfeiters at that time.

77 *Guido, Alessandro, or their brother:* the Guidi family, Counts of Romena.

78 Branda was a spring near Romena, not the same as Branda Fount in Siena.

80 Guido died before his brothers.

97 In Genesis 39 is told the story of Potiphar's wife, who, after Joseph rejected her overtures, falsely accused him to her husband, saying he had tried to seduce her.

98 *Sinon:* the Greek who persuaded the Trojans to take his countrymen's hollow wooden horse within the city walls and so facilitate the Trojan defeat (see *Aeneid* II, 57ff.).

128 *Narcissus:* gazed at his reflection in a pool of water. The *Metamorphoses* (III, 407ff.) tell how he was transfixed by his own reflection until he died and became a flower.

CANTO XXXI / *Sharon Olds*

4 *lance:* The magic spear of Achilles and Peleus could both wound and cure; it alone could heal the wound it made.

59 *pine cone:* a gilt bronze pine cone, ten feet tall, then located in the courtyard of St. Peter's.

63 *Frisians:* Teutons noted for their height. Apparently Dante pictures them standing on each other's shoulders.

67 *Raphel may amech zabi almi:* unintelligible language.

77 *Nimrod:* the ruler of Babel at the time of the building of the tower (Genesis 10:8–10 11:2–9, 6:4).

94 *Ephialtes:* (along with Briareus, 98) piled mountains on top of one another to try to reach the gods.

101 *Antaeus:* a Libyan wrestler whose strength was renewed whenever he was thrown down upon his mother Earth.

114 *ell:* a measure, chiefly for cloth, thought to be about one yard.

116 *Scipio:* Scipio Africanus Major, Publius Cornelius, third century B.C. Roman general who invaded Africa and defeated Hannibal.

123 *Cocytus:* tributary to the Acheron.

124 *Tityus, Typhon:* giants (mentioned in Lucan's *Pharsalia*).

136 *The Garisenda:* a leaning tower in Bologna.

CANTO XXXII / *Deborah Digges*

11 *Thebes:* initially a city of royal houses, became a place of crime and corruption. Dante seems to be drawing a parallel between the history of Thebes, its initial greatness and denigration, to the "shades," their original ambitions and betrayals, who dwell in the Ninth Circle. Dante, like Amphion, calls on the Muses to help him tell the story of Caina and Antenora. Dante frames this canto, here at the beginning, and also near the end, by references to Thebes.

12 *Amphion:* the son of Zeus, and a musician. He and his brother Zethus once took up the task of fortifying Thebes by building a wall around it. Amphion was weaker than his brother and could not move the stones. The Muses assisted him as he played his lyre, and the stones from Cithaeron followed Amphion's music down the mountain.

29 Pietrapana mountain, known today as La Pania, is in Tuscany. Tambernic cannot be identified. It may have been part of a mythical landscape of which Dante knew.

31 The frog is the first of many references to animals in this canto. Most of these references find equivalents and/or resonance in the Old Testament's Genesis and Exodus.

41 Two brothers, Alessandro and Napoleone, are the first two traitors to family introduced in Canto XXXII, to be followed by many others. As Camicion de'Pazzi narrates, their father was called Alberto. Alberto owned land in the Bisenzio river valley. The brothers fought over their inheritance and killed each other.

59 *Caina:* from Cain, introduced in Genesis, Chapter 4—is the utmost region of Cocytus. This is where traitors to family are punished.

61 This reference to Arthur recalls his slaying of Mordred. The story goes that Arthur's blow to his nephew was so fierce that when he pulled away his lance, one could see daylight through the wound; Mordred's shadow was thus, at the heart or center, illuminated.

63 *Focaccia:* of the Cancellieri of Pistoia. He murdered relatives for political gain.

65 The speaker here, "who had lost his ears to the cold," recalls, for Dante, Sassol Mascheroni of Toschi of Florence, who, like Arthur, murdered his nephew, but over a dispute concerning an inheritance.

68 The narrator of this passage, Camicion de'Pazzi, is not known, though the Pazzi were noblemen in Tuscany. It is believed that Carlino, for whom Camicion de'Pazzi claims to be waiting, is nephew to the former. Carlino was traitor to a castle that the Florentine Whites held in 1302. Thus, Carlino will be sent, according to de'Pazzi, to Antenora, the lower circle, wherein traitors to country are punished.

79 At the Battle of Montaperti, Bocca degli Abbati, the head who refuses to give Dante his name, cut off the hand of a Florentine.

117 *Buoso da Duera:* in charge of the Ghibellines in 1265, he was sent out to oppose the passage of one of Charles of Anjou's armies. But Buoso da Duera accepted a bribe and let the French pass.

119 *Beccheria:* a Church official who plotted with the exiled Ghibellines. He was beheaded in 1258.

121 *Gianni de' Soldanier:* a traitor to his political party. He became a leader of the Guelphs.

122 *Ganelon:* (met in Canto XXXI) a traitor to Roland, one of Charlemagne's knights.

124 Opening the city gates to allow Faenza to be overrun by the Bolognese Guelphs, Tebaldello betrayed Ghibelline refugees.

130 *Tydeus:* one of the seven Kings who attacked Thebes. Menalippus mortally wounded him and gnawed at his head in an act of revenge.

CANTO XXXIII / *Robert Hass*

13 Ugolino della Gherardesca, Conte di Donoratico, was born around 1220 to a traditionally Ghibelline family. He allied himself in various power struggles with the Florentine Guelphs, and, after a life full of political intriguing, he was arrested by the Ghibelline Ruggieri, then chief magistrate of Pisa, and locked with two of his sons, Gaddo and Uguiccione, and two of his grandsons, Anselmo and Nino, called "il Brigata," in the prison that came to be known as the Torre della Fama, the Hunger Tower. Ugolino had been imprisoned for nine months when the order was given to seal the door.

14 Ruggieri degli Ubaldine was archbishop of Pisa from 1278 to 1295. He is supposed to have lured Ugolino into the trap in which he was arrested by arranging a conciliatory meeting.

31 The Gualandi, Sismondi, and Lafranchi were Ghibelline families of Pisa.

75 *Poscia, piu che 'l dolor, pote 'l digiuno:* Some commentators have thought that this line implies not that Ugolino died at last, but that he was driven to eat the flesh of his children, and the grammar doesn't absolutely rule out the possibility. The strongest argument for such a view is that Ugolino, otherwise, is treated as a figure of immense pity, which is inappropriate to the culminating portraits of human evil in the *Inferno.* I think the issue is not, despite the various scholarly arguments, finally decideable on linguistic or philosophical grounds, which means that readers will have to decide for themselves whether this poignant parent-sorrow survives in the coldest, filthiest, most malicious reaches of Hell—or whether the capacity for lying, denial, and self-pity have survived there mixed unreadably with the most intense dolor. In either case it should be clear to readers that Ugolino's lifetime of scheming and treachery is what put his boys where they were and that, in his hatred for Ruggieri, he seems not to have registered that fact. In this sense, at least, he did cannibalize his children.

80 In Provence *yes* was *oc*, in northern France *oil*, in Italy *si*.

82 *Capraia and Gorgona:* islands north of Corsica near the mouth of the Arno. They belonged to Pisa.

89 *Thebes:* a byword for civic bloodletting.

118 *Friar Alberigo:* of the Manfredi family, Guelphs of Faenza. He had a relative and political rival Manfredo and his son killed at a banquet at his house. He is supposed to have signaled the assassins by calling for the fruit course.

120 Dates were much more expensive than figs.

124 *Ptolomea:* the third part of Cocytus where those who have betrayed guests are punished.

126 *Atropos:* the one of the three fates who cuts the thread of life.

137 *Ser Branca d'Oria:* born ca. 1233 and died ca. 1375, a member of a Ghibelline family of Genoa. He murdered his father-in-law, Michele Zanche of Sardinia (see Canto XXII), at a banquet to which he invited him.

143 *Malebranch:* the fifth *bolgia* of the Eighth Circle of Hell, the place where Church graft is punished.

CANTO XXXIV / *Robert Hass*

1 In the first line Virgil is quoting from a sixth-century hymn written in Latin by Venantius Fortunatus, Bishop of Poitiers: *Vexilla Regis prodeunt.* It means, "The banner of the King appears, or proceeds." The King is Christ and the banner is the Cross. The hymn was sung during Passion Week. Virgil alters the line for its present application: *Vexilla regis prodeunt inferni.*

20 *Dis:* a name for Pluto, the god of the underworld, used by Virgil in the *Aeneid.*

38 The three faces correspond to the Trinity.

62 *Judas Iscariot:* the apostle who betrayed Christ.

65 Marius Junius Brutus was one of the assassins of Julius Caesar. Gaius Cassius Longus was another. Both committed suicide when their coup failed.

89 *Lucifer:* "light-bearer," one of the names of Satan.

112 In Dante's conception the earth is round, the area of dry land is in one hemisphere with Jerusalem at its center, and the other hemisphere is a sea from which the mountain of Purgatory rises. Here the travelers have passed through the center of the earth and have entered the depths of the southern hemisphere.

115 The man who lived without sin was Jesus Christ.

117 *Judecca:* the last subdivision of Hell, named for Judas. According to Charles Singleton, the name was also commonly used "for the ghetto in which Jews were confined in European cities."

128 *Beelzebub:* the name given in the gospels to the chief of devils.

130 The stream is possibly Lethe.

139 Both the Purgatorio and Paradiso also end with the word *stelle,* or stars.